Wolfgang Hauke

The Transformation of the Class Culture into a natural Democracy of symbiotic Equal Rights

FSC
www.fsc.org
MIX
Papier aus verantwortungsvollen Quellen
Paper from responsible sources
FSC® C105338

Wolfgang Hauke

The Transformation of the Class Culture into a natural Democracy of symbiotic Equal Rights

Bibliographic information of the German National Library: The German National Library lists this publication in the German National Bibliography; detailed bibliographic data can be accessed on the Internet via http://www.dnb.de.

Herstellung und Verlag: BoD – Books on Demand, Norderstedt

ISBN: 978-3-75975-843-9

Table of contents

Chapter 2
The constitution of a natural democracy of symbiotic equal rights

Chapter 3
The biological philosophy

Introduction

People today find themselves in a cultural dilemma. On the one hand, it is becoming increasingly clear that man can no longer afford to 'carry on as before'. On the other hand, his supernatural cultural organisation has become so complex that he cannot change it radically without risking a cultural crisis. Therefore, there is no other realistic solution than the targeted transformation of the current culture into a natural democracy of symbiotic equal rights.

This book not only traces how man has ended up in today's cultural situation but also shows a way in which man can systematically realise a natural democracy of symbiotic equal rights.

Chapter 1
The present cultural constitution and its adverse effects on human and earthly nature

The nature of the present state constitution

One of the most influential political theorists during the Enlightenment was Thomas Hobbes (1588-1679). He was of the opinion that mankind needs an absolutist polity. Thomas Hobbes considered this absolutist polity, which he called Leviathan, to be the only way for mankind to organise itself in a sustainable way. By 1600 A.D., class culture had come to cultivate an unnatural, sado-masochistic relationship system through which constant relational warfare had become 'normal' in the culture, so Thomas Hobbes had developed the conviction that man was incapable of maintaining long-term peace. In his opinion, only a threatening, omnipotent polity was therefore able to protect mankind from self-destruction.

As Thomas Hobbes' views found broad acceptance within the society of his time, many of his ideas were incorporated into the development of a new state constitution in the 18th century. The provisional result of this development today is an absolutist state, which is realised through a constitution and three organisational pillars: a legislature (legislative power), a judiciary (judicial power) and an executive (civil service). To this day, this has become a sham democracy that reduces the direct political influence of ordinary people to an electoral process that takes place every four years. After each round of elections, there is a leap in authority from the bottom to the top, so that the culture is governed from top to bottom in an absolutist manner until the next election.

This cultural organisation harbours several dangers for modern man, which only become clear on closer inspection. Within today's class culture, a dictatorial relationship has normalised between the absolutised state and its citizens. The state is able to assert itself in an absolute manner primarily because the official apparatus that regulates modern cultural life is not elected by the citizens. Since such a state organisation prevents the realisation of a real democracy, the cultural citizen remains relatively powerless within today's class culture. This powerlessness is underpinned by 3 organisational pillars of the state constitution:

1. The state's taxes are collected through a so-called 'non-affective' tax collection base. This means that the citizen cannot expect any specific state benefits in return for their tax payments. This means, for example, that the taxes that citizens pay for their cars or for an intact road transport network can be used for any other government purpose. The executive thus has a free hand in the use of tax revenue and can theoretically also use the tax money for a better control of the citizens.

2) The state's monopoly on the use of force creates an absolutist political sovereignty within the culture, so that

the state can eliminate any resistance by citizens against the state at any time by using police or military force.

3) The legal principle of 'positive law before natural law' applied in modern states was invented in the Roman Empire in order to be able to involve the numerous slaves in daily legal transactions. 'Positive' law is therefore to be understood as an arbitrarily established law through which the state can override natural human rights and also enact legally valid laws that are directed against human nature. A 'positive' jurisprudence can therefore align itself like a flag with the prevailing political winds in society, so that what is still right today can become wrong relatively quickly.

The dangers of 'positive' jurisprudence became particularly evident through the Jewish laws of the Third Reich, so that after the Second World War a solution was sought for the political vulnerability of 'positive' legal practice. However, the apparent solution of applying the so-called 'Radbruch formula' by Gustav Radbruch (1878-1949) did not eliminate the Achilles' heel of traditional jurisprudence. The formula stipulates that people must abide by positive law in any case, but that the judge is required to suspend positive law as soon as a positive law generates an intolerable injustice.

This dubious rescue of 'positive law' depends on the strong personality of the adjudicating judge and is not subject to any clear legal regulation. As a result, the recommendation of Radbruch's formula always falls short in legal practice.

People can achieve effective protection against a cultural jurisprudence that is becoming inhumane above all if they transform the traditional cultural basis of jurisprudence 'positive law before natural law' into the basis of jurisprudence 'natural law before positive law'. Only in this way can natural human rights be effectively anchored within a culture.

A state constitution that organises itself through 'non-affective' tax collection, through an absolutist monopoly on the use of force and through 'positive' jurisprudence can become a despotic dictatorship within a relatively short period of time. As a result, the situation of the citizens of an absolutist state constitution remains fundamentally uncertain and is always determined by the political currents in the culture.

In his book 'Psychology of the Masses' [1] published in 1895, Gustave le Bon writes the following about a rapid derailment of state power: [...] 'In 'The Individual against the State' [1884], Herbert Spencer [1820-1903] says the following about the English Parliament: 'Legislation has taken the course I predicted. Dictatorial measures, rapidly multiplying, are constantly endeavouring to restrain personal liberty in two ways: Every year an ever-increasing number of legal requirements are enacted that impose restrictions on the citizen's former freedom of action, forcing him to do things he could previously do or not do at will. At the same time, more and more oppressive burdens, especially local taxes, have from the beginning limited his liberty, by diminishing that part of his income that he could spend at pleasure, and increasing

1. Citation: Gustave le Bon, Alfred Kröner Verlag Stuttgart, 1911, S149 f

that part that was taken from him to be spent according to the good will of the officials.'

This ever-increasing restriction of liberty is manifested in all countries in a particular way to which Spencer did not allude: The creation of those innumerable legal measures of a generally restrictive nature necessarily leads to an increase in the number, power, and influence of the officials charged with their execution. They have therefore every prospect of becoming the true masters of the countries of civilisation. Their power is all the greater because only the caste of civil servants, the only one that is unaccountable, impersonal and employed for life, escapes the incessant change of power. But there is no tyranny harsher than this one, which appears in this threefold form. The constant creation of laws and restrictive measures, which surround the most insignificant expressions of life with Byzantine formalities, has the disastrous result of increasingly narrowing the area in which the citizen can move freely. Victims of the fallacy that an increase in laws would better secure freedom and equality, the people only take upon themselves more oppressive shackles. They do not take them on with impunity. Accustomed to bear every yoke, they eventually come to seek it out, and in the end forfeit all originality and vigour. They are nothing but insubstantial shadows, automatons, without will, without resistance and strength. If man can no longer find the vigour within himself, he must seek it elsewhere. With the increasing indifference and powerlessness of citizens, the importance of governments must only grow. They must, of necessity, possess the spirit of initiative, enterprise and leadership that citizens have lost. They have to undertake, manage and protect everything. Thus the state becomes an omnipotent god.' [...]

This description resembles today's cultural development in an astonishing way, which is why it suggests that the absolutist state has been producing very specific cultural symptoms and developmental phenomena since the 19th century.

Neil Postman (1931-2003), professor of communication studies, commented on the modern state bureaucratic machine in his book 'The Technopoly '[2] in the following way: The transformation of bureaucracy from a set of procedures serving social institutions into an autonomous meta-institution that largely obeys its own purposes was the result of various developments that took place around the middle and towards the end of the 19th century: rapid industrial growth, improvements in transport and communications, an expansion of state activities into ever wider sectors of public and economic life, and the increasing centralisation of state and administrative structures. Added to this in the 20th century was the information explosion and what could be described as the 'bureaucracy effect': As the techniques for managing information became more necessary, more widespread and more complex, the number of people and structures required to manage these techniques increased, as did the amount of information that these bureaucratic techniques in turn generated. Thus a need arose for bureaucracies to direct and coordinate the existing bureaucracies, then a need for additional structures and techniques to direct

---

2. Citation: „ Das Technopol“ Neil, Postman, S. Fischer Verlag GmbH, 1992, S.51 f

those bureaucracies, which in turn coordinated bureaucracies, and so on - until finally, to paraphrase Karl Kraus' remark about psychoanalysis, bureaucracy became the disease it claims to be the cure for.

In the course of this development, it ceased to be a servant of social institutions and became their ruler. Today, bureaucracy not only solves problems, it also creates new ones. More importantly, it defines what our problems are - and from the bureaucracy's point of view, these are always efficiency problems. This makes bureaucracies extremely dangerous, as C. S. Lewis says, because while they were originally only intended to deal with technical information, today they are called in to deal with ethical, social and political problems. The bureaucracy of the 19th century was concerned with the more efficient organisation of transport, industry and the distribution of goods. The bureaucracy of the technopoly has freed itself from such restrictions and today claims supremacy over all aspects of society.'

As a rule, the modern man of culture does not have a sufficient understanding of the way in which he is integrated into the state to which he belongs. A certain idea of this integration is made clear by the administrative law of the civil service apparatus in the Federal Republic of Germany, which is described in the book 'Grundriß des Verwaltungsrechts '[3]. The following quotations speak for themselves and enable the reader to make a certain assessment of his situation as a citizen:

---

3 Quotes: „Grundriß des Verwaltungsrechts“, Andreas Wittern, Verlag W. Kohlhammer, 1990

P. 19 f. [...] 'The state and every other holder of public authority is fundamentally and by its nature superior to the citizen. However, they do not always make use of their special powers and their position as sovereigns. It often 'descends from its height' and places itself on a level with the citizen in order to conduct legal transactions with him as an equal. This is how one distinguishes between sovereign and fiscal administration.' [...]

P. 15 f. [...] Administration is all state activity that is neither jurisdiction nor legislation, [= executive] While the legislature creates more or less rigid norms that are detached from individual cases and determined for the long term, and while jurisdiction retrospectively judges completed life processes according to these norms and decides disputes that have arisen, it is typical of the administration that it has to practically realise the will of the state, the diversity of life for the good of the community; to this end, it must act with foresight and preventively, it shapes the daily reality of community life'. [...]

P. 16 [...] 'An essential characteristic of the administration is that it may and must act not only when and because the law commands it, but on its own initiative and by virtue of its own sovereign function. As an equal-ranking part of state authority, it must form and exercise an independent sovereign will. In doing so, it may not overstep the bounds of the law, but it also does not require an explicit legal command to act. The administration is not just an 'extended arm'! It is not merely an executive organ of the legislator, but can and must do what is necessary for the community on its own initiative. For example, the establishment of a register of traffic offences was permissible even though no law expressly ordered or permitted this' (BverwG in NJW 56, 357)[...]

P. 45 [...] In contrast to the general parts of civil law and criminal law (Book 1 of the German Civil Code and the Criminal Code) [...], general administrative law is not codified in a coherent manner. While the administrative procedure - albeit scattered in various laws - has found statutory regulations, the rules of substantive general administrative law are not to be found in written law, apart from a few [...]. Here, administrative practice, administrative jurisprudence and, in particular, administrative case law have filled the existing gaps with unwritten principles (according to BverwG in DVBI.57,392). Large parts of general administrative law therefore belong to customary law.' [...]

[...] No matter how unlawful a VA [administrative act] may be, no matter how unpleasant it may be for the person concerned, no matter how necessary the action of the authority may appear to the citizen; he can only obtain the cancellation of the VA or the action of the authorities by way of legal action if his subjective public right is violated by the behaviour of the authority. The concept of subjective public law is not universally valid and abstract, but changes with changing political, ideological and social views. In its current form, the concept serves, among other things, to delimit the citizen's rights of control over state measures and, in particular, to exclude the so-called popular action, an action with which the citizen should be able to challenge any state measure in court. [...]
P. 60 [...] In public law, the legal obligation of a public

authority to do something often does not trigger a söR [subjective public right] of the individual to fulfil this obligation. There are in fact numerous provisions that oblige the authorities to do something that is favourable to all or individual citizens, but without granting them a right to fulfil the obligation towards the authorities (and thus a claim against them). [...]

The excerpts from the 'Grundriß des Verwaltungsrechts' make it clear how one-sided the bureaucratic regulations are for the citizen in the FRG and how little the FRG citizen can rely on the granting of officially conceded rights. Today, more or less all citizens of Western civilisation are affected by this problem.

The history of capitalism

In the 15th century, the European nations began to realise 'liberal' colonialism and imperialism, which gradually spread to the whole world. The establishment of the British and Dutch East India Companies at the beginning of the 17th century led to a veritable 'liberal-parasitic', sadistic and sometimes tyrannical exploitation of colonial peoples. This ultimately gave rise to so-called 'free trade', which has remained obligatory for the nations of the '1st, 2nd and 3rd world' to this day and continues to result in unnatural and asocial cultural symptoms.

The industrial revolution that began in Europe in the 18th century was organised in the tradition of 'free trade' through the exploitation of slaves and the creation of a new type of working-class proletariat. Since the turn of the millennium, this new form of imperialism and colonialism, which also has an impact on nations, has led to the establishment of progressive capitalism, which is increasingly taking on people in a holistic way.

Karl Polanyi (1886-1964), a Hungarian economic historian, vividly traced the history of the development of capitalism in his book 'The Great Transformation '[4]:

P.110 ff. [...] 'The more complicated industrial production became, the more numerous became the factors of production whose existence had to be secured. Three of these were [...] of the utmost importance: labour, land and money. In a commercial society, availability could only be guaranteed in one way: by making it purchasable. It therefore had to be organised in such a way that it was for sale on the market, in other words, that it was considered a commodity'.

[...] 'One of the three factors stands out in particular: labour power is the terminus technicus for people insofar as they are not employers but employees. It follows that from then on the organisation of labour had to adapt to the developments of the market system. But since the organisation of labour is merely another name for the forms of life of the common people, this means that the development of the market system had to be accompanied by a change in the social organisation itself. In the course of this development, human society had degenerated into an accessory of the economic system.'[...].

---

4. Quotes: Karl Polanyi: The Great Transformation Politische und Ökonomische Ursprünge von Gesellschaften und Wirtschaftssystemen, Suhrkamp Verlag, 1978

P. 224 ff. [...] 'To separate labour from other activities of life and to subject it to the law of the market means to extinguish all organisational forms of being and to replace them by another form of organisation, an atomistic and individualistic form. Such a destructive scheme is best served by applying the principle of freedom of contract. In practice, this means that non-contractual forms such as kinship, neighbourhood, profession and confession had to be liquidated, since they demanded loyalty and devotion from the individual and thus restricted his freedom. If this is presented as the principle of non-interference, as the supporters of economic liberalism used to do, it was nothing other than the expression of a deep-rooted, [...] certain kind of interference, namely one that was intended to destroy the non-contractual relationships between people and prevent their spontaneous re-formation.

This effect of establishing a labour market is clearly visible in colonial territories today. The natives are to be forced to earn their living by selling their labour. To this end, their traditional institutions must be destroyed and their re-establishment prevented, since in a primitive society the individual is not usually threatened by hunger as long as the community as a whole does not fall into this situation. In the Kral land system of the Kaffirs, for example, impoverishment is impossible: Whoever needs help receives it unconditionally. No Kwakiutl has ever been in danger of going hungry. There is no hunger in societies that have the necessities of life.

The principle of freedom from want was equally observed in the village community of India, and, let us add, also in almost every and every kind of social organisation of

Europe till about the beginning of the 16th century.' [...] 'It is precisely the absence of the threat of individual hunger that makes primitive society in a certain sense more humane than market-economy society.'[...]

'Grotesquely enough, the white man's first contribution to the black man's world consisted mainly in familiarising him with the possible applications of the scourge of hunger. Thus the colonists could think of cutting down the breadfruit trees to create an artificial food shortage, or they could impose a tax on the huts of the natives to force them to sell their labour'[...].

[...] 'What the white man perhaps still practices today in remote regions, namely the breaking up of social structures in order to squeeze the element of labour out of them, was done to white populations by white men in the 18th century for similar purposes. Hobbes's grotesque image of the state as a human leviathan whose vast body was composed of an endless number of human bodies was eclipsed by the construction of the labour market in Ricardo's sense, a stream of human bodies whose supply was regulated by the amount of food made available to them. Although the existence of a general standard below which no worker's wage could fall was recognised, it was thought that this limit would only be effective if the worker was faced with the choice of either having nothing to eat or offering his labour power on the market at the price offered.

This incidentally explains an otherwise inexplicable omission of the classical national economists, namely why only the fear of hunger, but not the attraction of higher wages, was ascribed the ability to create a functioning labour market. Here, too, developments in the colonies confirmed their experiences. The higher the wages, the lower the incentive to perform for the native, who, unlike the white man, does not feel compelled by his cultural norms to earn as much money as possible.

This analogy was all the more striking because the early labourer also feared the factory, where he felt humiliated and tortured, like the native, who could often only summon himself to work in our way if he was threatened with corporal punishment, if not mutilation.

The factory owners of Lyon in the 18th century advocated low wages mainly for sociological reasons. Only an overworked and downtrodden labourer, they argued, would refrain from joining forces with his fellow workers in order to escape the condition of personal serfdom, under which he could be forced to do whatever his masters demanded of him. Legal coercion and parish slavery as in England, the hardships of an absolutist labour police as on the European continent and contract labour as in early North and South America were the preconditions for the 'willing worker'. The final stage, however, was reached with the application of 'nature's punishment', hunger. In order to be able to utilise it, it was necessary to liquidate the organic social order, which would not allow the individual to starve.'[...]

P. 120 f. [...] 'The reform of the Poor Law in 1834 [in England] removed this obstacle to the labour market: the 'right to subsistence' was abolished. [...] If the Speenhamland system [= English poor relief. Author's note] had prevented the emergence of a working class, the labouring poor were now united into such a class by the pressure of a callous mechanism. If, under the Speenhamland system, people were cared for in a way that animals would not be expected to be, they were now expected to care for themselves, with all the odds stacked against them.

If the Speenhamland system brought about a kind of sheltered misery, now the labouring man had become homeless in his own society.
Where the Speenhamland system had made excessive demands on the values of neighbourhood, family and rural environment, man was now detached from home and family from all roots and any harmonious environment.
In short, if the Speenhamland system meant the rottenness of immobility, the danger now was death by exposure.'[...]

The following remarks by Karl Polanyi can be better understood with the knowledge that Joseph Townsend (1739-1816) summarised the theories of Thomas Hobbes (1588-1679), Thomas Robert Malthus (1766-1834) and David Ricardo (1772-1823) into a new economic formula of faith. This gave rise to an extremist, anti-social economic philosophy, which over time ensured that the humane national economics of Adam Smith (1723-1790) was given less and less consideration.

With the capitalist bourgeoisie turning to the views of David Ricardo, Thomas Robert Malthus and Joseph Townsend, Adam Smith's doctrine was considerably modified and finally completely alienated in its essence by the reversal of the natural exchange formula 'commodity-

money-commodity' into the new exchange formula 'money-commodity-money'.
By reversing the natural exchange formula into the money-commodity-money exchange formula, money was declared to be the actual meaning and purpose of 'liberal' capitalism, so that profit and gaining power became the absolutist guidelines of the capitalist economy. The consequence was that 'liberal' capitalism no longer had any regard for human nature or the nature of the earth.

Karl Marx recognised the nature and consequences of this new formula of 'liberal' capitalism and described it in his work 'Das Kapital'. [5] He was a contemporary witness to the effects of the new economic formula of money-commodity-money on society, which slowly but surely led to a 'liberal-parasitic', sado-masochistic and tyrannical industrial revolution. This revolution had no qualms about exploiting young children as young as 4 years old for heavy mining labour and polluting the natural environment in any way it saw fit.

Since capitalism created the obligation for all people to perform supernatural labour to secure the basic means of survival, what the worker had to do in real terms to make a living was increasingly increased. In the 19th century, for example, weavers repeatedly found it difficult to survive despite a 16-hour working day. This liberal-capitalist process of progressively intensifying exploitation of workers became so acute in the late 19th century that the first massive labour movement formed in all Western cultures.

---

5. http://ciml.250x.com/archive/marx_engels/german/kapital1.pdf Das Kapital S.96 f.

Karl Polanyi analysed and documented this historical development:
P. 161 [...] 'Hobbes had argued for the necessity of a despot, since men are like animals. Townsend, on the other hand, maintained that they were indeed animals and that for this very reason only a minimum of government was necessary.' [...]

P.159 f. [...] [Townsend quote] 'Hunger tames the wildest beasts, it teaches even the most recalcitrant decency, politeness, obedience and subordination. In general, hunger alone will spur and guide them (the poor) to labour, and yet our laws have prescribed that they should never go hungry. Admittedly, the laws have also prescribed that they should be induced to labour. But legal compulsion involves so much trouble, violence and noise, creates bad blood and can never produce good and useful service. Hunger, on the other hand, not only exerts a peaceful, silent, and unceasing pressure, but is also the most natural cause of diligence and labour, and thus produces the greatest possible exertion, and, when satisfied by the free magnanimity of others, lays the permanent and firm foundations of good will and gratitude. The slave must be compelled to labour, but the free man should have the right of his own judgement and discretion; he should be protected in the enjoyment of his property, whether it be much or little, and he should be punished if he encroaches on his neighbour's property.'

'This was a new starting point for political science. By looking at human society from the animal side, Townsend bypassed the supposedly unavoidable question of the foundations of rule and thus introduced a new concept of law into human affairs, namely that of the laws of nature.' [...]

Karl Polanyi's remarks make it clear that the parasitic and tyrannical mentality of colonial and imperial 'free trade' has intensified in a 'progressive' way as a result of the Industrial Revolution. This gave rise to an asocial economic philosophy and 'liberal' capitalism, for which not only wage slavery but also the ruthless exploitation of nature became a matter of course.

To this day, this 'mentality' of 'liberal' capitalism has not changed significantly. The capitalist belief in a self-regulating capitalist market that requires no supervision by society therefore still exists today.
In this respect, Adam Smith spoke of a 'divine hand' within the economy. A closer look at capitalist history, however, reveals that 'the market' has been dominated by the hand of corporations since the early 20th century at the latest.

Karl Polanyi answered the capitalist belief formula of a self-regulating market in his own way: [...] 'We argue that the idea of a self-regulating market means a crass utopia. Such an institution could not exist over long periods of time without destroying the human and natural substance of society.' [...].

In this statement, Karl Polanyi was referring to the world wars of the 20th century, for the emergence of which he held the 'liberal' capitalism' of the 19th century responsible. From 1890 onwards, capitalism had led to progressively escalating economic and military competition between European states, so that the First World War had a devastating effect on European culture as a whole.

The danger of social disruption caused by capitalist 'free trade' has once again become acute for people today since 1985 as a result of the policies of Ronald Reagan and Margaret Thatcher and the 'Washington Consensus'. This is because the agenda of 'liberal capitalism' from the 19th century has been revived and globalised.

Neoliberal capitalism since 1985

From 1950 onwards, a new mass production emerged within the '1st world' through so-called 'Fordism. '2 As a result, many economic groups reached the economic scale of modern states in the 1970s. This led to a change in the content of the hitherto prevailing economic theory views, which ultimately led to a shift towards the economic theories of the so-called Chicago School and in particular the theories of Milton Friedman. This ultimately revitalised the 'liberal' capitalism of the 19th century within the '1st world'.

In 1985, the so-called 'Washington Consensus' led to a new policy for lending to 3rd world countries and thus to a strong promotion of a global 'neoliberal' cultural agenda, which was far more favourable to the interests of American and European corporations. As a result, all the insights and conclusions that mankind had drawn from the drastic lessons of the 20th century were ultimately suppressed and discarded.

How dangerous the neoliberal agenda has become for people today can be measured above all by the fact that neoliberalism only judges people according to their usefulness for a constant increase in economic power. Such an instrumentalisation and functionalisation of man puts 'The Economy' first and declares it a saviour, so that 'The Market' becomes a sacred cow. If a modern person accepts such an economic religion, the perverse view that man is there for the economy and not, as is the case within a natural community organisation, the economy for man, becomes normalised in him.

Since neoliberalism still regards social expenditure merely as a cost to be minimised in the pursuit of neoliberal profit and power, the modern citizen does not count as a human being for neoliberal culture, but only in his cultural and economic functions as a voter, worker, taxpayer and consumer. For a neoliberal economic corporation and a neoliberal state, it therefore makes no difference what religion, skin colour or gender a person has. Both human nature and human character are irrelevant to the neoliberal agenda, which is purely focused on profit and power. As a result, the neoliberal agenda has caused an increasing asocial decomposition of society to this day, which is slowly but surely transforming modern man into a materialistic lone wolf.

The agenda of a progressively increasing global economic power is still being created today through the absolutist occupation of a living space with the help of the supernatural capitalist concept of property. Today, the neoliberal 'investor' uses the absolutist concept of property in the best possible way, as this allows him to gain centralised power of disposal over all natural assets on earth. He is supported politically and legally by the neoliberal organisations of the IMF (International Monetary Fund) and the World Bank, which have been active since 1985, and by the WTO (World Trade Organisation) since 1995.

Neoliberal hoarding of more and more property by fewer and fewer owners necessarily means a progressive restriction of natural property on earth. As a result, the offence of biological theft is sometimes committed as soon as a family in the 'third world', which has farmed a certain piece of land for generations, is driven off its land overnight because a neoliberal corporation or a neoliberal state has obtained a title to this land.

The general natural right of all natural individuals to occupy a certain territory by virtue of their natural self-will and to defend it against intruders also applies to people in the 'third world', whose land has often been owned by their families for many generations. However, neither the natural right of ownership nor traditional customary law can assert themselves against the supernatural property invented by class culture as an arbitrarily absolutised possession created by 'positive law'. Thus, with regard to the process of concentration of global property in the hands of fewer and fewer people that has been taking place for around 40 years, we can speak of an organised theft that is legalised by an arbitrary 'positive' right of ownership.

The current abundance of power of the master race is based, on the one hand, on the capitalist concept of property and, on the other, on the moral and social degeneration of modern society through a materialistic individualism that has become 'normal'. The neo-liberal media industry ensures that the 'ordinary' person sees the resulting global concentration of wealth, which is becoming increasingly explosive, and the resulting increasing cultural pressure to exist as necessary and 'swallows' it.

We can therefore speak of a progressive global takeover of power by the modern economic and financial aristocracy, which began in 1985 with an about-turn in Western politics and the 'Washington Consensus' and which is to be completed by Agenda 2030. As a result, mankind is once again heading towards a disastrous cultural crisis.

In his book in 1944, Karl Polanyi described the explosive cultural situation created by 19th century 'capitalism'. This description is strikingly similar to today's cultural situation:
'The bourgeoisie was the bearer of the emerging market economy; its business interests, as far as production and employment were concerned, coincided by and large with the interests of the general public.' [...] 'On the other hand, the classes engaged in trade and commerce had no sense of the dangers arising from the exploitation of the worker's physical strength as well as from the destruction of family life, the devastation of neighbourly relations, the deforestation of forests, the pollution of rivers, the decline of craftsmanship, the decay of folk customs and the general decline of life.'[...]

'The bourgeoisie fulfilled its task by developing an almost sacramental faith in the general blessings of profit, but this disqualified it as the guardian of other interests equally important to a good life.'[...]

The discussion makes it clear that the tragic economic development of the 19th century and its consequences are currently being repeated in many respects. It is therefore important for people today to realise how dangerous it can be for people today to blindly listen to and trust the cultural authorities of today's class culture.

The Communist Manifesto

The ideological root of political communism can be found above all in the Communist Manifesto by Karl Marx and Friedrich Engels [6]. The Communist Manifesto contains an abridged version of the history of class culture and an analysis of the effects of 'liberal' capitalism on human self-organisation in the 19th century.

P. 21 [...] 'The history of all hitherto existing society is the history of class struggles. Freeman and slave, patrician and plebeian, baron and serf, guild burgher and journeyman, in short, oppressor and oppressed stood in constant opposition to each other, waging an uninterrupted, sometimes hidden, sometimes open struggle, a struggle that ended each time with a revolutionary reorganisation of the whole society or with the common downfall of the fighting classes. [...]

P. 23 [...] 'The bourgeoisie, where it has come to power, has destroyed all feudal, patriarchal, idyllic relations. It has

---

6. Das Kommunistische Manifest Ausgabe 2008 https://www.ibiblio.org/ml/libri/e/EngelsFMarxKH_ManifestKommunistischen_p.pdf

ruthlessly torn asunder the colourful feudal ties which bound man to his natural superior, and has left no other bond between man and man than naked interest, than the unfeeling 'cash payment'. It has drowned the holy shivers of pious ardour, of chivalrous enthusiasm, of philistine melancholy in the ice-cold water of selfish calculation. It has dissolved personal dignity into exchange value and replaced the countless vested and well-acquired freedoms with an unscrupulous freedom of trade. It has, in a word, substituted open, impudent, direct, arid exploitation for exploitation cloaked in religious and political illusions.
The bourgeoisie has stripped of their halo all the hitherto venerable and piously revered activities. It has transformed the doctor, the lawyer, the clergyman, the poet, the man of science into its paid labourers.' [...]

[...] 'The bourgeoisie's need for an ever-expanding market for its products chases it over the entire globe. Everywhere it must nestle, everywhere cultivate, everywhere establish connections. Through its exploitation of the world market, the bourgeoisie has cosmopolitanised the production and consumption of all countries. To the great regret of the reactionaries, it has pulled the national soil of industry out from under their feet. The ancient national industries have been destroyed and are still being destroyed daily. They are being supplanted by new industries, the introduction of which is becoming a question of life for all civilised nations.[...] The bourgeoisie is dragging all nations, even the most barbarous, into civilisation by the rapid improvement of all instruments of production and by infinitely facilitated communication. The cheap prices of its commodities are the heavy artillery with which it shoots all Chinese walls into the ground, with which it forces the most obstinate xenophobia of the barbarians to capitulate. It forces all nations to adopt the bourgeoisie's mode of production if they do not wish to perish; it forces them to introduce so-called civilisation into themselves, i.e. to become bourgeois. In a word, it creates a world in its own image.' [...]

P. 26 [...] The bourgeois relations of production and transport, the bourgeois relations of property, modern bourgeois society, which has conjured up such enormous means of production and transport, is like the sorcerer who is no longer able to control the subterranean forces he has conjured up. For decades, the history of industry and commerce has been nothing but markets. By what, then? By preparing more all-round and more violent crises and by diminishing the means of preventing them.' [...]

P. 26 [...] 'To the same extent that the bourgeoisie, i.e. capital, is developing, to the same extent is the proletariat developing, the class of modern workers who live only as long as they find work, and who find work only as long as their labour increases capital. These labourers, who must sell themselves piecemeal, are a commodity like any other article of commerce and are therefore equally exposed to all the vicissitudes of competition, all the fluctuations of the market. The labour of the proletarians has lost all independent character, and therefore all attraction for the workers, through the extension of machinery and the division of labour. [...]

P. 48 f. [...] 'The first attempts of the proletariat to directly assert its own class interest in a time of general agitation, in the period of the overthrow of feudal society, necessarily failed because of the undeveloped form of the proletariat itself as well as because of the lack of the material conditions for its liberation. [...] The revolutionary literature that accompanied these first movements of the proletariat is necessarily reactionary in content. It teaches a general asceticism and a crude egalitarianism'. [...] 'Since the development of the class antagonism keeps pace with the development of industry, they find just as little the material conditions for the liberation of the proletariat and search for a social science, for social laws to create these conditions. Social activity must be replaced by their personal inventive activity, the historical conditions of liberation by fantastic ones, the gradual organisation of the proletariat into a class by a specially devised organisation of society'. [...] 'They want to improve the living conditions of all members of society, including the best-off. They therefore constantly appeal to the whole of society without distinction, indeed preferably to the ruling class'. [...] 'Gradually they fall into the category of the reactionary or conservative socialists described above and differ from them only in their more systematic pedantry, in their fanatical superstition in the miraculous effects of their social science.' [...] [This also applies to the party of today's Left, author's note].

The critical passages in the Communist Manifesto

In addition to the general analysis of economic history, we also find several extremist passages in the Communist Manifesto that indicate an allergic reaction of the authors to the bourgeoisie of their time. As a result, some passages in the Communist Manifesto favoured disastrous cultural developments:

P. 31 [...] The proletarians can only conquer the social productive forces by abolishing their own previous mode of appropriation and thus the whole previous mode of appropriation. The proletarians have nothing of their own to secure, they have to destroy all previous private securities and private insurances. All previous movements were movements of minorities or in the interests of minorities. The proletarian movement is the independent movement of the immense majority in the interests of the immense majority. The proletariat, the lowest stratum of present society, cannot rise, cannot rise up, without blowing up the whole superstructure of the strata that make up official society.' [...]

This passage necessarily unsettled many people and contributed to the fact that, with the advent of Fordism from 1950 onwards, more and more workers distanced themselves from the communist doctrine and the labour movement.

P.36 [...] 'Abolition of the family! Even the most radical are enraged by this shameful intention of the communists. What is the present, bourgeois family based on? On capital, on private acquisition. Fully developed, it exists only for the bourgeoisie; but it finds its complement in the enforced familylessness of the proletarians and public prostitution. The family of the bourgeois naturally disappears with the disappearance of this complement, and both disappear with the disappearance of capital. Do you accuse us of wanting to abolish the exploitation of children by their parents? We admit this crime'[...].

In principle, the dissolution of the family is a catastrophic event for children because, unlike animals, they go through an extremely complex 18-year maturing process during which they need constant guidance, support and protection from a family group. A family can therefore be supplemented, but not replaced, by a communist community.

P. 38 [...] 'The communists have also been accused of wanting to abolish the fatherland, the nationality. The workers have no fatherland. One cannot take from them what they do not have. In that the proletariat must first conquer political rule, elevate itself to a national class, constitute itself as a nation, it is itself still national, even if by no means in the sense of the bourgeoisie.' [...]

Every natural community of people needs its own country, just as animals and plants need their own territory. We can therefore change the term fatherland, but not what the members of a nation emotionally associate with their country and their people. The sense of home that people develop for the immediate environment in which they grow up gives them a feeling of safety and security that is important for their emotional well-being. The significance that such a sense of home can achieve is made particularly clear by the fact that people can become downright sick with homesickness.

P. 38 [...] 'The national separations and antagonisms of the peoples disappear more and more with the development of the bourgeoisie, with the freedom of trade, the world market, the uniformity of industrial production and the living conditions corresponding to it. The rule of the proletariat will make them disappear even more.

Modern science has sufficiently confirmed that life on earth is realised through the individual, so that no two flies are alike. Life as such is therefore realised in a creative way and through relative freedom. The realisation of industrial mass animal husbandry or cultural mass human husbandry for mass production and mass consumption more or less cancels out natural creativity and freedom and therefore has corresponding unnatural consequences for society as a whole.

P.40 [...] 'We have already seen above that the first step in the workers' revolution is the elevation of the proletariat to the ruling class, the struggle for democracy. The proletariat will use its political rule to gradually wrest all capital from the bourgeoisie, to centralise all instruments of production in the hands of the state, i.e. the proletariat organised as the ruling class, and to increase the mass of the forces of production as rapidly as possible. At first, of course, this can only be done by means of despotic interventions in the right of property and in the bourgeois relations of production, i.e. by measures which appear economically inadequate and untenable, but which in the course of the movement outstrip themselves and are unavoidable as a means of overturning the whole mode of production'. [...]

Where this idea has led is made clear by the self-organisation of China, which since 1985 has cultivated a mixture of political dictatorship by the Communist Party and 'liberal' capitalism. As a result, Chinese citizens today are effectively controlled by 600 million cameras and dictated by the 'constraints' of a digital system of rewards and punishments.

P. 52 [...] 'The Communists disdain to conceal their views and intentions. They openly declare that their purposes can only be achieved by the violent overthrow of all previous social order. Let the ruling classes tremble before a communist revolution. The proletarians have nothing to lose in it but their chains. They have a world to win. Proletarians of all countries, unite'[...].

The hope for a violent revolution has never been satisfactorily fulfilled in cultural history, since all violent revolutions have a destructive development trap. As soon as the revolutionaries use the same supernatural power as the current rulers of the class culture to remove the cultural rulers, they inevitably enter into a process of dissolving their natural framework of social behaviour. As a result, despite their initial good intentions, over time the new rulers develop no less absolutist and tyrannical behaviour than the rulers removed by the revolution. This transformation also took place in Russia under Lenin, leading to the Stalinist gulag era under communism, which cost the lives of around 20 million people.

The relative approach of communist theory

Karl Marx and Friedrich Engels were children of their time, the time of the heyday of idealism, which was characterised above all by the after-effects of the philosopher Friedrich Hegel (1770 - 1831 AD).

Karl Marx was one of the few who did not apply Hegel's idealistic methods, as he drew his conclusions from analysing everyday cultural reality. As a result, he tended to follow the cosmogony of Aristotle (pragmatism) and not the cosmogony of Plato (idealism):

'My dialectical method is not only fundamentally different from Hegel's, but its direct opposite. For Hegel, the thought process, which he even transforms into an independent subject under the name of idea, is the demiurge of the real, which only forms its external appearance. For me, conversely, the ideal is nothing other than the material realised and translated in the human mind'. (MARX, MEW 23, P. 27).

Despite these clear words, Karl Marx's tendency to react allergically to the bourgeoisie favoured an aberration of his followers into an idealistic Marx 'ism' and commun 'ism'. As a result, the theories of Karl Marx and Friedrich Engels ultimately became an absolutist political religion or an 'opium for the people'.

Karl Marx himself did not describe himself as a Marxist. 'All I know is that I am not a Marxist.' (MEW 37, P. 436),

Friedrich Engels also wanted the common model of thought to be understood not as a dogma but as a guide to action. We find these natural objectives confirmed by the following quotations from Karl Marx and Friedrich Engels: 'In general, the word “materialist” serves many younger writers in Germany as a simple phrase with which one labels everything and anything without further study, i.e. one sticks this label on and then believes to

have dismissed the matter. Our conception of history, however, is above all a guide to study, not a lever of construction a la Hegelianism.
The whole of history must be studied new, the conditions of existence of the various social formations must be examined in detail before an attempt is made to identify the political, private-legal, aesthetic, philosophical, religious etc. ways of looking at things that correspond to them. The political, private-legal, aesthetic, philosophical, religious, etc. views that correspond to them must be derived from them. Very little has been done in this respect up to now, because only a few have seriously endeavoured to do so.

We could use masses of help in this, the field is infinitely large, and those who want to work seriously can achieve a great deal and distinguish themselves. Instead, however, the phrase of historical materialism (you can turn anything into a phrase) serves many younger Germans only to systematically correct their own relatively meagre historical knowledge - economic history is still in its nappies! - to systematically construct their own relatively meagre historical knowledge - economic history is still in nappies!' (Engels MEW 37 p. 436-437)

'The question of whether human thought is capable of objective truth is not a question of theory, but a practical question. In practice, man must recognise the truth, that is, the reality and power, the worldliness of his thinking.' (Marx, MEW 3 p. 533)
"The foundation of irreligious criticism is: Man makes religion, religion does not make man. Religious misery is in one sense the expression of real misery and in another

the protest against real misery. Religion is the sigh of the oppressed creature, the spirit of a heartless world, as it is the spirit of spiritless conditions. It is the opium of the people". (Marx, MEW 1 p. 378)

'As philosophy finds its material weapons in the proletariat, so the proletariat finds its spiritual weapons in philosophy, and as soon as the lightning of thought has struck thoroughly into this naive popular soil, the emancipation of the Germans into human beings will take place.' (Marx MEW 1 p. 3911)

We can conclude from these quotes that Karl Marx and Friedrich Engels were inspired by an empathetic spirit. However, in the face of the degenerating capitalist and political cultural conditions of their time, both were repeatedly caught up in allergic reactions, which were also very clearly expressed in harsh fantasies of retaliation. As a result, access to communist theory became an ideological stumbling block for many people, which favoured the emergence of absolutist communist thinking in the formation of a materialist substitute religion.

The communist ultimate goal of a classless society cannot be achieved by force, as such a path contradicts the natural nature of human beings. At best, a deliberate but moderate transformation of human consciousness and the human worldview towards a biological worldview can ultimately lead to a natural democracy of symbiotic equality, which corresponds to Marx and Engels' vision of a classless society.

The cultural caused development of addiction

Modern class culture has become so unbearable for many people that those affected develop a strong desire to live in a better world in their 'free time'. This better world can be, for example, the exercising of a sport, a journey in imaginations or an excursion into the virtual world of television and the Internet.

Above all sensational experiences can make people forget their everyday lives. As a result, modern man has developed a relative weakness for a supernatural and sensational entertainment and has learnt to 'switch off' the reality as soon as he 'switches on' a television or computer.

Such an unnatural psychological survival formula is not without consequences, as human nature generates a habituation effect that, over time, transforms all experiences that were once exciting and thrilling into something ordinary. As a result, those affected either have to increase the dose of their sensational entertainment or consume it at ever shorter intervals in order to achieve a sufficient distraction effect from everyday reality. In this way, many of those affected fall into the trap of psychological dependency and develop an addiction to supernatural and sensational distractions and entertainments.

Through their addiction development, those affected search for ever new sensational experiences that have a 'kick effect' on human nature, until they finally realise that their addiction is having a destructive effect on their behaviour and on their mental, emotional or physical well-being.

Even the simple medicine in the Middle Ages was aware that the dose makes the poison, so that too much of something is just too much. This even applies to salt, which is essential for human life, as an overdose of salt can also be lethal.

The real problem with substance-induced addictions is therefore not the kick drug itself (cocaine, marijuana, alcohol, cigarettes, coffee, sweets, etc.), but the intensity of the cultural unbearability felt in each case, which the individual tries to neutralise. The dose of supernatural distractions and sensational kicks that a person needs for this depends on their social environment, how acceptable their job is and how their partnership and family relationships turn out. The more unbearable a person finds their life, the more likely it is that the distractions from this feeling will lead to a destructive addiction.

Many modern people have developed a veritable kick-logistic, through which they keep the dose of their different distractions within limits. The corresponding complex of artificial stimuli, motivations and distractions can only be maintained for a certain period of time. Since the cultural man finds his life also unbearable because he can only fulfil his natural needs to a limited extent within a class culture, the inner pressure to find a sufficient solution to this problematic situation does not cease and repeatedly causes aggressive states of mind. These bouts of aggression can be directed against other things, living beings and people as well as against themselves and sometimes result in excessive drug use.

Many man therefore develop a special, non-substance-related addiction, the addiction to war games. This form of effective distraction through an 'aggression hygiene' works primarily because the human brain works according to the WYSIWYG principle. (What You See Is What You Get - what you see is reality). As a result, war games on the computer, regardless of whether they are designed in the style of comics or realistically, can trigger strong kick effects in players and at the same time reduce inner aggression. The addiction to war games is therefore far less harmless than most people assume today, as it tends to rob those affected of a big part of their daily time more than most other addictions. Hours of excessive computer gaming have a degenerative effect on the mental, emotional and physical condition of those affected through the law of natural economy. This natural economic effect is made particularly clear by the example of a broken leg that has been in plaster for weeks and shows significant muscle atrophy after the plaster has been removed. All natural abilities that man do not or only rarely use are reduced accordingly by the natural economy, even if they are vital abilities.

Today's class culture cultivates a particularly intense media world of distraction, which reduces the philosophy of many people to a Roman 'bread and games' or a modern 'pizza and war games' policy. Such an agenda, which becomes an addiction, leaves little room for important biological life experiences and for the development of important social abilities .

In view of the massive cultural distractions from the unbearable political and social realities of everyday life, people should therefore not be surprised that the social relationships of cultural man have become increasingly factual, shallow and superficial since the turn of the millennium.

Many people today try to neutralise their feelings and their chronic lack of natural satisfactions by automating their work, consumer and relationship behaviour. As a result, the thoughts and actions of those affected are increasingly controlled by fixed habits organised by the cerebellum. Over time, these habits become as natural to people as walking, which is also coordinated by the cerebellum in the form of automatic action sequences.

As it is the task of the cerebrum, but not the cerebellum, to critically analyse and constructively shape one's own behaviour, the cerebellum also automates destructive human behaviours if this is not prevented on the part of the cerebrum.

If a person therefore realises at some point that their habitual behaviours, emotions and thought impulses have become too destructive, it takes a certain amount of time for the cerebellum to stop generating the destructive habits automatically. It therefore proves to be beneficial if those affected do not fight the habits they have recognised as unfavourable, but instead develop and pursue new behaviours that can be 'ingrained' in the cerebellum through a special emphasis and a conscious repetition. This allows those affected to leave their destructive habits to the natural economics, which degrades everything that is no longer in use over time. In order to consciously change one's own behaviour, it is therefore important to go initially through a difficult phase of reorganisation until the new behaviours have become established and the old behavioural habits have been broken down.

Anyone who recognises the logistics of natural habit formation can also understand that any culturally determined behavioural habit that has a destructive inner consequence can become dangerous for people.

The power of media

We know from the latest scientific research that the human brain has different operating states. The so-called half-sleep is of particular importance. As hypnosis has shown us, the cerebrum is partially blanked out in a state of half-sleep. As a result, a person can sometimes be so strongly influenced by external messages through hypnosis that they are transformed into a puppet hanging on the silken strings of someone else's will. Even 'switching off' in front of the television harbours a certain risk, depending on the respective state of fatigue, of people being unconsciously influenced by the media content.

As the human brain functions according to the so-called WYSIWYG principle (What You See Is What You Get - what you see is reality), the television content consumed influences the human psyche in a fundamental way. As soon as a person resorts to the social ability of empathic identification whilst television, they can fade out their natural self and slip into the role of an actor. How dangerous such temporary selflessness can become depends above all on the quality of the television

programme. If a viewer identifies with actors from the 'sex, drugs and crime' film genre, consciously or unconsciously imitating these roles in everyday life can distort their natural social behaviour in a detrimental way. Children in particular are not yet able to deal properly with 'liberal' media content and prevent any effects of the television programmes on their own behaviour. Children are in a constant learning mode as they have to master the major task of developing their own world view. To do this, they copy the human behavioural roles in their respective environment in order to experiment with them. If a young child therefore watches too much television, there is a risk of lasting ideological and emotional contamination.
Such contaminations can often no longer be corrected by the parents.

The dangers of targeted media influence

Since a person cannot enter into a personal relationship with all the people of another people, human thinking transforms all peoples, countries, counties, cities and communities into a metaphorical I. This makes it possible to generate a simple abstract reference to all communalisations. Therefore, when two peoples conclude a contract, human consciousness recognises each people as a separate I-contracting party in which, symbolically speaking, 'all stand for one'.

This particular ideological self-organisation of people offers the demagogues of the class culture the possibility for a targeted media manipulation of society. For example, by the systematically inciting hatred against another people and using an absolutist friend-foe polarisation, a demagogue can put an entire people under supernatural tension and trigger an enthusiastic approval for a war. Such propagandistic enthusiasm for war is not covered by a real war, since in war the individual is confronted with real fellow human beings whom he is supposed to kill, although no one has done anything concrete to the other.

The harmless identification of a person with a community therefore always ends where his influence on the community ends. The more people unite to form a community, the more superficial the individual's relationship to the masses becomes and the easier the people are swept along by professionally generated emotional affects such as a surge of enthusiasm.

The citizens of modern class culture are particularly susceptible to such stimuli, as culture undermines all social-symbiotic human relationships for the successful organisation of its absolutist cultural machines. As a result, the normal cultural citizen is relatively easy to influence through strong social sensations and communal experiences.

The propaganda

The realisation that the thinking and behaviour of the modern peoples can be directed by media manipulations led to the emergence of so-called propaganda in the 20th century. The foundation stone for the mass propaganda, which today we also refer to as 'public relations', was laid in 1928 by Edward Bernay. In his book 'Propaganda', he developed a systematic agenda, sometimes seemingly embarrassing to today's readers, for the 'self-evident' influence of cultural authorities on ordinary cultural people.

After the Second World War, the methods of 'public relations' in both politics and business were increasingly potentiated and expanded through the so-called 'social engineering'. Thereby the thinking and the behaviour of modern peoples was changed through broad social, political and economic interventions in culture with a massive support of the media.

The neoliberal shock strategy in particular, which can psychologically paralyse the entire people for a certain period of time through shocking messages or sudden changes in culture, has proven to be effective. If the paralysis disappears again, it is usually too late to take action against the changes that have already taken place in the culture, as new cultural realities have been created in the meantime that cannot be easily reversed.

It is therefore important for people today to condemn this kind of influence on their lives in a fundamental way so that they do not become a puppet hanging on the silken strings of the will of the cultural 'authorities'.

The television and its effects

In the book 'On Television' by Pierre Bourdieu, we find an interesting summary of the effect of modern news programmes on the viewer: [...] '[News programmes are often reduced (ed.)] to an incongruous sequence of events that have nothing to do with each other and are merely brought together, an earthquake in Turkey, the idea of cuts in the state budget, a victory in sport and a sensational trial, and which are completely reduced to absurdity by being cut off from their entire history and their consequences.' [...].

[...] 'This de-historicised and de-historicising, atomised and atomising view finds its paradigmatic expression in the image of the world presented by television news: a succession of seemingly absurd stories that ultimately all resemble each other, uninterrupted marches of peoples abandoned to misery, a sequence of events that emerged unexplained, will disappear unresolved, today the Congo, yesterday Biafra, tomorrow Sudan, and which, stripped of any political inevitability, are at best capable of triggering a vague humanitarian interest. ' [...]

[...] 'The victims, unlike those affected by train derailments and other accidents, are not suited to provoke political solidarity or indignation. It is therefore entirely within the logic of the journalistic field, particularly through its particular form, [...] to produce an image of the world in which history appears as an absurd series of incomprehensible and uninfluenceable disasters. This world, overflowing with ethnic wars and racist hatred, violence and crime, is so incomprehensible and frightening that one can only retreat from it and seek safety.'

[...] 'Xenophobic fears are fuelled, just as the deceptive impression that crime and violence are constantly on the rise reinforces the anxieties and phobias that feed security thinking. The feeling that the world as shown on television is beyond the handle of ordinary mortals is combined with the impression that the political game, like professional sport with its sharp distinction between practitioners and spectators, is a matter for professionals.' [...]

Neil Postman, a professor of communication studies also analysed the effects of television in a critical way in his book 'The Disappearance of Childhood'1:

P. 113 [...] 'Marshall McLuhan was once asked why the news on television was always bad news. He replied that this was by no means the case; The television advertising brings the good news.

And that is indeed the case. It's comforting to know that you can recover from the daily grind with a trip to Jamaica or Hawaii, that you can raise your status by buying a Cordoba, that you can become a better housewife by using a certain detergent, that you can increase your sex appeal with a certain mouthwash. Such are the promises of American culture, and they lend a certain conclusiveness to the motivations of adults'. [...]

P. 121 [...] 'On a randomly selected WCBS show in one evening, it looked like this: 264 seconds for a story about the corruptibility of politicians; 37 seconds for a related story about Senator Larry Pressler; 40 seconds about Iran; 22 seconds about Aeroflot; 28 seconds about a massacre in Afghanistan; 25 seconds about Muhammad Ali; 53 seconds about a prison riot in New Mexico; 160 seconds about protests against the film Cruising; 18 seconds about the owners of the discotheque Studio 54; 18 seconds about Suzanne Somers; 16 seconds about the Rockettes;

This way of defining 'news' has two significant implications. Firstly, it makes it difficult to think about an event; secondly, it makes it difficult to develop feelings about an event.

P. 123 f. [...] 'One must remember that television news shows are almost surrealistic - disjointed to the point where nothing can be related to anything else. What is the connection between Aeroflot and Suzanne Somers? Between 'Studio 54' and Iran? Between a cruise and a massacre in Afghanistan? Are any of these incidents being followed up? Were they also newsworthy yesterday? Why is Iran worth 40 seconds and the St John's game 166? And finally, how do the commercials relate to the other stories?

[...] There were 21 commercials on the WCBS show, totalling about ten minutes. Three of them preceded the bribery story, four preceded the prison riot in New Mexico. As you can imagine, the adverts were optimistic, promising satisfaction, security and, in two cases, erotic pleasure. What kind of picture are we supposed to form of reality in the face of this juxtaposition and confusion? How should we assess the importance of events? The television news show has a single, consistent answer to all these questions: a sense of proportion cannot be recognised in the world. Each event stands on its own; the past and the history are irrelevant; there is no reason to value one fact over another. ' [...]

P. 131 [...] 'Most of [television's] content is expressed in images, not in language. And therefore they must necessarily dispense of a discussion. Hence the almost inexhaustible power of television to entertain. It is the first real theatre of the masses, not only because it reaches a huge number of people, but also because almost everything on television takes the form of a story, a narrative, rather than an argument or a sequence of ideas. Politics becomes a story; news becomes a story; business and religion become a story. Even science becomes a story.'

Here Neil Postman describes one of the main reasons why, shortly before the turn of the millennium, many people began to largely block out the past and the future from their thinking in order to concentrate on the here and now. This here and now is no longer analysed and evaluated and therefore remains a relatively indifferent, positivistic here and now. This massive change in personal self-organisation has led to a change in media policy, which Neil Postman describes in his book 'The Technopoly'[7] .

P. 182 f. [...] 'By the turn of the century, advertisers were moving away from the view that reason was the best instrument for disseminating products and ideas. From then on, advertising consisted of one part depth psychology and one part aesthetics. In the course of this development, a fundamental principle of capitalist ideology fell by the wayside: namely that both the producer and the consumer are involved in a rational process in the course of which the consumer makes his choice on the basis of a careful examination of the quality of a product and taking his own interests into account. At any rate, this is what Adam Smith had in mind. But today, television advertising is hardly about the character of a product. It is about the character of the person consuming the product. Images of film stars, celebrity athletes,

---

7. Book: Neil Postman „ Das Technopol“ S. Fischer Verlag GmbH, 1992

peaceful lakes, macho fishing trips, elegant dinners and romantic rendezvous, happy families packing their station wagons for a picnic in the country - none of this says anything about the products being sold. But it says everything about the fears, fantasies and dreams of those who are supposed to buy them.

The advertiser does not need to know what qualities his product possesses, he needs to know where the defects and weaknesses of those who are to buy it lie. That is why less and less is being spent on product research and more and more on market research. In other words, the economy has reorientated itself: its primary goal is not the good product, but the consumer who feels good. Doing business has become a pseudo-therapy and the consumer a patient who is given a sense of calm and security through psychodramas.' [...]

Neil Postman summarises his research on the media at the end of the 1990s in the following way:
P. 183 [...] 'Somewhere near the centre of the technopoly, then, there is a vast industry that takes the liberty of making all available symbols subservient to the interests of business by devouring the psyche of consumers. The numbers vary, but a conservative estimate is that an American has seen about two million commercials on television by the age of sixty-five. If we add to that the number of radio spots, newspaper and magazine adverts and billboards, it is fair to say that the overload of symbols, and with it their emptying of meaning, has reached an unprecedented level in human history.' [...] 'The inhibitions are so low that we can speak of a cultural rape, sanctioned by an ideology that gives unlimited

priority to technical progress and is completely indifferent to the decomposition of tradition.' [...]

The arbitrary branding

Since the turn of the millennium, many corporations have built their business on targeted branding, so that the image of a company is placed in the foreground. A corresponding public relations, which link a company logo with arbitrary positivistic ideas and associations, promote certain ideas and moods in consumers which, after some time of the constant repetition, are automated by the cerebellum. As soon as the consumer sees a familiar company logo, the cerebellum reactivates the stored ideas and associations with this logo in a reflexive way in the human consciousness.

Since the mid-1990s, corporations have been using this recognition effect to interfere in the personal self-organisation of modern man with arbitrary and supernatural media messages. This results in a particular 'shopping addiction' based on positivistic and hedonistic associations and emotions. The luxury consumption fuelled by this sometimes makes modern people stubbornly blind to the long-term social and biological damage caused by such ultimately unjustified and superfluous consumption.

Modern people today must therefore pay very careful attention to their habits of action and behaviour, as constant media stimuli can condense into particular views and habit formations that are automated by the human cerebellum, even before those affected are aware of the long-term consequences of these views and habit formations.

The Roman media policy

Today's media implement a traditional Roman power agenda that aims to polarise the citizen's self-organisation in an absolute way through a supernatural fear on the one hand and a supernatural enthusiasm on the other. As a result, those affected by media consumption largely ignore their innate relative nature and adapt in a relatively unnoticed way to a media agenda that polarises the thinking and behaviour of cultural people in an unnatural way.

Through the constant refinement of media technology and the increasingly effective utilisation of accumulated psychological knowledge since the turn of the millennium, modern media have become so effective that the culture of class is no longer dependent on traditional cultural religion to maintain its supernatural constitution upright.

Only this realisation gives the observer a realistic impression of how powerful and dangerous modern media politics has become for mankind. One symptom of this increased power that has so far gone relatively unnoticed is the increase in the number of people who perceive a moderate, natural behaviour as 'boring'. Those affected by this consider both the bottomless fear kick and the bottomless enthusiasm kick to be 'normal'. As a result, they lose sight of the entire lively spectrum of the natural centre and are at considerable risk of suffering from medial self-poisoning.

Chapter 2
The constitution of a natural democracy of symbiotic equal rights

The first chapter of the book makes it clear that for a transformation of today's culture into a natural democracy of symbiotic equal rights overcoming material problems is of secondary importance. Today's human beings primarily need a natural cultural vision and a biological philosophy of life that can serve as a guideline for the realisation of a natural self-organisation and a healthy community organisation.

One source for such a guideline is the science of ethnology, which has studied numerous naturally organising communities and their habits of life over the last 150 years. Therefore, when it is spoken of a natural way of life, natural behaviour or natural social organisation in the following, this refers to the findings of ethnology and other scientific fields of research that deal with the self-organisation of human and earthly nature.

The natural political equilibrium and the human striving for security and freedom

Within a natural community organisation, politics can be defined as the effort to balance the natural interests of human nature in order to achieve a balanced social and symbiotic self-organisation:

1. The I interests = the empathic reference to one's own existence, the mental, emotional and physical self-preservation and the cultivation of personal talents and interests.

2. The YOU interests = the cultivation of companionships, friendships, partnerships and family relationships.

3. The WE interests = the constructive cultural affinity, the empathic connection with all life and the development of a holistic world view.

To achieve this, both the small village and the large state must take into account the mutually complementary aspirations of all people for security and freedom in an appropriate manner.

For around 100 years, people have known that the universe and nature on earth are organised by dynamic interrelationships of a relative kind. In addition to a dynamic polarisation of the universe through a relative order (security) and through a relative chaos (freedom), we find the natural electricity on earth with its + and - polarisation, the phenomenon of high and low tide and also a dynamic polarisation of the human sense of taste, e.g. through the taste dynamics of sweet and sour.

If, for whatever reason, a person strives for absolute security through an absolute order, he tragically excludes natural freedom from his endeavours and becomes an opponent of freedom, since he sees freedom only as an not welcome unsecurity in his life. The same applies to a human striving for absolute freedom, for which every natural order becomes an obstacle. As soon as a person therefore makes his relative natural needs and views absolute, the natural alternating poles of life within his self-organisation no longer complement each other, but are mutually exclusive. A unnatural ideological self-organisation of the absolutist kind can therefore have an extremely fatal effect on the self-organisation of a person, a village or an entire society.

Even after 100 years of the theory of relativity, modern cultural man still organise himself in an absolutistic way by holding on to the 2400-year-old ideological concept of so-called idealism. Platonic idealism (Plato 427-347 BC) assumes that absolute divine ideas exist in the universe, which underlie all living phenomena on earth as models. As a result, the 'perfect' divine ideas are considered to be of higher value than the realisation of these ideas through an 'imperfect' biological existence. The idealist therefore regards all living beings on earth, including humans, as inferior images of 'higher' divine ideas.

Through idealism, a hierarchical division of spirit, soul and body has been established within the ideological self-organisation of class culture, which humans still integrate in their worldview und realise in a relatively unconscious way in their everyday cultural life. The tendencies to overvalue all human ideas, observations and goals, to doubt and criticise the emotions and to devalue the body are correspondingly destructive. A further consequence of this arbitrary categorisation of humans life is that man has been relatively ruthless in his treatment of the earth's nature for 2000 years.

The idealistic organisation of the human world view has produced numerous ideological 'ism' complexes in Western cultural history, such as material 'ism', which make a questionable claim to absolute, idealistic, divine and universal validity. As a result, many people still fanatically adhere to one 'ism' belief complexes today and defend them against all 'enemies' who represent a different 'ism' belief complex.

The ideological wars that continue to flare up today, for example between a capital 'ism' and a commun 'ism' and between the world religions, make it clear how stubbornly and with what destructive consequences man has clung to the ideological concept of idealism since Greek civilisation.

This also applies to the conflicts between a 'right-wing' and a 'left-wing' politic of the idealistic kind that have been rampant within modern class culture for around 100 years, which have arisen from the exaggerated desire for an absolute cultural order on the one hand (dictatorship, fascism, communism) and for absolute freedom on the other (anarchism). As a result, a veritable idealistic war has remained 'normal' within class culture to this day, polarising society in an absolutist manner and dividing it through hostile ideological camps.

Since the turn of the millennium, the neoliberal agenda has promoted this internal division through the modern media, thereby driving social cultural relations into a progressive decomposition. This decomposition became virulent or bottomless after the stock market crisis of 2008, so that since then all natural viewpoints of man have

been progressively dissolving and giving way to an increasingly bottomless idealistic arbitrariness.
The result is a subterranean yet fierce ideological and emotional war within society, which most people today no longer know how it came about or whether it makes any sense.

People today can end this ideological war within their culture primarily by consciously reflecting on a natural worldview with relative views and always bearing in mind that the relative poles of the natural order and the natural freedom complement each other and are not mutually exclusive. By slowly but surely reducing the ideological tendency towards idealism and absolutism, man can ensure that the politics is no longer an idealistic theatre of war, but once again becomes a biological art for the balanced satisfaction of the natural human needs of I, YOU and WE.

The contradictory polarisation of personal self-organisation through absolutist selflessness and absolutist egocentricity

For around 5000 years, all class cultures insist on the adaptation of the cultural human being to the military machine, the economic machine and the bureaucratic machine of culture through an ideal of the absolutist selflessness. This unnatural selflessness was idealised in Western culture by the Roman Catholic Church and by the Protestant religious forms in such an emphatic way that absolutist social selflessness has remained a norm of

behaviour passed down through the generations in all Western cultures to this day.
For 70 years, the materialistic religion of 'liberal' capitalism has demanded an egocentric material self-organisation from the cultural citizen in order to keep the capitalist economic machine of modern class culture running.

For this reason, an idealistic polarisation has arisen within the personally self-organisation of modern man through the contradictory ideals of an absolutist social selflessness and an absolutist materialist egocentricity. Without being aware of this sufficiently, cultural man are always in the danger to develop an inner idealistic contradiction of the schizophrenic kind.

This also applies to current cultural policy, which blindly demands too much selflessness from citizens and at the same time tries to cultivate a neoliberal economic policy of a bottomlessly egocentric kind.
This political schizophrenia, which is still cultivated by the media, can be canceled by modern man by relativising his tendencies towards an absolutist social selflessness and an absolutist materialistic egocentricity and by inserting conciously for a balanced natural I-organisation, YOU-organisation and WE-organisation.

The modern systems research and the natural heterarchical self-organisation

From the middle of the 20th century onwards, modern science became increasingly concerned with a new scientific discipline known as systems research. Thereby the complex self-organisation of the higher mammals and the ecological niches was examined with regard to their respective internal constitution. Thereby the terms 'autopoietic, multistable and heterarchical multilevel organisation' were coined to describe the model of the specific natural self-organisation.

The natural system organisation can be characterised by three main features:

1. The so-called autopoietic ability to spontaneously self-ignite from seemingly nothing within favourable environmental conditions, to develop a systematic order and to generate a self-sufficient reproduction

2. An internal system balance of efficiency (effectiveness) and elasticity (flexibility)

3. A heterarchical multi-level organisation, which differs qualitatively from the hierarchical organisation in that the individual organisational levels organise themselves in a relatively independent manner.

In order to better understand the internal balance between the efficiency and elasticity of a natural system, a concrete example is helpful. If a person has a whole network of friends, he can fall back on his other friends for support in the event of an attack by one of these friends. This enables them to cope relatively well with social conflicts. The fewer symbiotic relationships a person has, the greater the impact of negative external interference on them and the lower their internal stability.

People today are generally not sufficiently aware of the importance of the elasticity of a system organisation, as neoliberal capitalism unilaterally overemphasises efficiency in all cultural fields. As a result, the social networking within the modern world of work and within the public sphere is reduced to a minimum in a dangerous way. The result is a relative instability of today's workplaces, communities and cultural fields and a general susceptibility of culture to social and political disruption.

A living system that manages itself through a heterarchical multi-level organisation constitutes superimposing levels of organisation, each of which organises itself in a relatively self-sufficient manner. This form of natural self-organisation becomes more tangible through a concrete example of a culturally organisation: Within a heterarchical society organisation, citizens would form the lowest level of organisation. In contrast to today's hierarchical society organisation, for which people elect a top leadership every four years, the citizens of a heterarchical social organisation would primarily elect their village and city officials, so that they remain in direct contact with these officials.

The elected administrative officials would form the second heterarchical organisational level and would not only perform their municipal tasks in a relatively independent manner, but would also elect the district officials from their ranks. This makes the 2nd organisational level of local officials an important organisational interface between the citizen and the district administration, which synchronises the respective interests of the citizens and the district administration with each other.

This heterarchical organisational system would continue with the district officials electing the land officials and the land officials electing the federal officials. This would create a direct natural line of legitimisation of the executive from the bottom to the top, so that all organisational levels remain connected to the organisational level below by a direct communication.

The main advantage of such a cultural organisation is that dictatorial cultural development is largely excluded. As the individual administrative levels each receive their legitimisation from below, the citizen has the first and last word in a heterarchical social organisation.

The natural economy

Around 10,000 years ago, humans began to organise themselves through a regular house economy in order to meet the daily food requirements of clan and tribal communities. Over time, this first human house economy was increasingly supplemented by simple bartering of food, handicraft products and luxury goods.

Today's global economy differs from this simple natural household economy primarily in that it produces a high level of luxury products for consumption that humans do not necessarily need. Since 1950, the economy is realising a mass production of luxury goods, which has led in the last 15 years to a progressive overloading of the earth's natural circulation systems.

In order for humans to be able to reduce this 'too much' in production to such an extent that it can fulfil the needs of human nature and earthly nature, it is helpful for humans to know how today's economy works and where humans can start today in order to slowly but surely reduce the production of luxury goods through a globally concerted action. It is not possible today to reduce economic production 'in one fell swoop', as the global economic networks and dependencies have already become too complex for this. A drastic cut in the current economic self-organisation could therefore trigger a serious global economic crisis.

The task of the naturally cultural economy

The naturally task of the cultural economy is to provide the human community with means of survival. This requires a marketplace for the many individual services and products that humans produce due to their creative and free nature, so that a regular exchange of these services and products can take place.

The resulting exchange market is self-regulating through the respective offers and the demand for these offers and remains constructive and progressive within a social and symbiotic cultural organisation. However, as soon as a culture realises a mass production and thus an unnaturally monotonous everyday working with relatively low pay and easily replaced workers, a supernatural economic pressure arises within the affected society. This pressure arises from the fact that the producer who increases his efficiency through mass production can offer his products at the expense of his workers more cheaply, than a producer who does not engage in unnatural exploitation of human nature.

In order to compete in a market that offers cheap mass products through unnatural and asocial production, all competitors must in the long run also implement an unnatural 'effective' exploitation of their workers or else exploit themselves in a supernatural way.

While in a healthy symbiotic culture the well-being of all remains the central goal of all economic activity, in an unnaturally class culture 'the market' determines market activity and drives both the economy and the entire social life of society into a progressive asocial distortion.

Only the social and symbiotic economy, which manages without the unnatural exploitation of people, can therefore be regarded as a sustainable and healthy economy for man.

Money, property and the capitalist credit system

In cultural history, money has always had the function of a neutral medium of exchange, for which early man mainly used shells, glass beads, livestock and other basic values recognised by his community. The use of money made it possible for the simple farmer to exchange his apples for a new wagon wheel without having to find a wagon wheel maker who was interested in apples. By exchanging apples for money and exchanging money for a wagon wheel, money became a neutral medium of exchange that has remained extremely advantageous for simple trade to this day.

With the invention of metal coins, money became both a medium of exchange and a neutral store of value, as coins cannot rot, break or die. By minting gold and silver coins, man has created a permanent supernatural value for himself, to which a corresponding aura still clings today.

After the first coins were used in Mesopotamia and Egypt, a veritable coinage and banking economy developed in Lydia in the 7th century BC, which was quickly adopted by the Greek city states. This led to an upswing in trade in Greece from 600 BC, which also led to the development of a financial and trading economy.

To this day, a relative balance between the existing money supply and the value of the goods and services produced in the cultural community has remained necessary for the sustainable use of money as an economic medium of exchange. An imbalance caused by an excessively high money supply leads to a devaluation of money (inflation) and an excessively low money supply leads to a devaluation of the products (deflation).

Maintaining the relative balance between the goods produced and the money produced is far easier to organise within a city state than within a nation state or within an entire association of states such as the European Union. For this reason, the amount of money in circulation today is regulated by state central banks or by the EU central bank.

One difficulty in correctly estimating and regulating the amount of money in circulation has arisen due to the increasing use of money as a store of value or a hoarding of money. Such a 'store of value' does not exist within the

natural economy of the earth, so we can speak of a supernatural cultural invention that makes the cultural economy susceptible to disruption in many ways.
The hoarding of wealth in the form of gold and silver has already led to an advanced supernatural concentration of power in culture in Mesopotamia and to a corresponding supernatural influence of the rich and powerful on the shaping of culture. As a result, the 'master man' of class culture developed an unnatural, bottomless striving for ever more wealth and power, which has repeatedly had a devastating effect on cultural history.

The supernatural property

Many people have not yet sufficiently understood the nature of today's cultural economy. This applies in particular to the special cultural invention of so-called property, which characterises today's cultural reality in a fundamental way.

The supernatural conception of property differs considerably from the nature of natural possessing. This becomes clear above all through the right of all living beings to take possession of a territory of life by virtue of their natural self-will. The natural right to occupy land and to claim the food that is available on this land is naturally limited to the specifically demarcated and marked territory and thus to a habitat that a living being actually uses. This is where the nature of natural possessing differs from the supernatural nature of the property, which embodies an absolutised claiming freed from all natural conditions.

Through the supernatural property created by class culture, man can now become the owner of a piece of land anywhere in the world that he neither occupies nor ever sees. This happens especially when the acquired land is merely an 'investment' that serves as a material life insurance. Through such a supernatural constitution of property, the culture of class necessarily declares the natural right of possession to be irrelevant.

For a property with a title to ownership, there is no longer any natural competition worldwide that can dispute the owner's ownership, even if the owner does not use the property at any way. Modern property is therefore an arbitrarily constructed absolutist possession of a supernatural kind, which has been supported and protected by the capitalistically organising Western states for 150 years. The absolutist property, which has remained obligatory in cultures to this day, is one of the main reasons why even after 100 years of the theory of relativity and even in the face of an increasingly overtaxed human and earthly nature, man continues to cling with all his might to the cultivation of a 'liberal' capitalist class culture.

Natural possession is divided within a natural community by an I possession (tools, clothing, sleeping place), a YOU possession (family territory, dwelling) and a WE possession (clans or tribal territory, community buildings, common tools). Organisational decisions for the use of natural possessions are made by a family council or by a joint council of heads of families. Such an organisation promotes a natural cohesion of the community, which is characterised by a mandatory sharing of natural possessions. This also extends in a relative way to the natural 'private property' of the individual. The social relationships and hospitality in the naturally organising families and communities are correspondingly pleasing and edifying.

As we can see more and more impressively today, the nature of supernatural property favors social isolation, absolutist commandments and prohibitions, an enormous loss of freedom through the demarcation of property territories with fences, and an antisocial personal egocentricity. Thereby the spiritual and emotional life of cultured people sometimes becomes extremely poor and without a sufficient empathy.

The historical beginnings of supernatural property

The beginnings of the realisation of property can already be found in the Mesopotamian 'high culture'. Since the Mesopotamian city-states have constantly waged wars over water rights on the Euphrates and Tigris rivers, the commanders of the city-states have been able to amass an enormous power. As a result the victorious military commanders levied the first time an absolutist claim to the lands conquered in a war. This development promoted a supernatural greed for possession and power in Mesopotamia, so that Sargon of Akkad founded a first great empire in Mesopotamia as early as 2350 BC, which included all of Sumer and parts of Asia Minor.

Since such absolutist power politics cannot be justified in a natural way, the military commander of a Mesopotamian city-state needed supernatural legitimation from the gods in order to be able to achieve a general cultural acceptance of his totalitarian claims to rule. As a result, in Mesopotamia, as well as in the advanced civilisations in Egypt and China, the former chief of the natural (primitive?) tribal communities, an absolutist god-king and from the former medicine man a high priest with a own priesthood, who became official governors of the gods on earth through an accordingly absolutist religious constitution.

This development remained questionable until today, since the chief and the medicine man held only relative offices for special rites and emergencies within the natural community organisation , such as in the event of an attack from outside or in the case of illness of tribal members. In this respect, anthropological researchers have unanimously confirmed that political decisions within natural communities are usually made by a council of male heads of families. The chief has the task of leading the respective discussions, but not the power to make decisions over the heads of the heads of the families.

In contrast, the invention of a God-King and an absolutist priesthood in the form of a governorship of the gods on earth was of a completely different, unnatural kind. These offices gave rise for the first time to a 'progressive' state system determined by an absolutist striving for power. This state was organised by a hierarchical military machine, by an absolutist economic machine and by an authoritarian bureaucratic machine, which became obligatory in the course of time. To this day, nothing has changed in this supernatural constitutional essence of class culture.

After Sargon of Akkad had conquered and united a first great empire, there was a constant war for supremacy in the Middle East. It happened more and more often that not only the conquered territories were incorporated into an already existing area of power, but also the defeated soldiers were turned into regular slaves. Until the emergence of the first Greek empire and the first slave markets in Greece, there was thereby a progressive, unnatural and anti-social cultural structure in the Middle East, the innermost essence of which was characterised both by the absolutist ownership of land and by the absolutist ownership of slaves without rights.

Today's property law should therefore still be treated with caution and can only be used with social and biological conditions without significant destructive side effects.

The emergence of capitalism from 600 BC onwards

From 600 BC onwards in Greece was developed a strong flowering of the natural house and barter economy and a first capitalist credit system. The basic idea for a capitalist credit system was that a lender would have sufficient security for lending his financial assets above all if two borrowing parties were willing to use their respective land as collateral for the loan. For the organisation of a loan agreement, a double collateralization of the scheduled loan amount by 2 borrowers or by a borrower and by a bank (Tempelbank) was therefore necessary.

Since the lender had to be granted not only a sufficient security pledge but also a reward for lending his money, interest was also invented as an ongoing fee for the duration of the loan agreement. Today's capitalism, which has become extremely complex, is based on a state-protected property, which is secured by the jurisprudence basis 'positive law before natural law'. This regulation has made it possible for the modern cultural bureaucracy to issue so-called value certificates, which can be handed over to today's lender as collateral. With this title value deed, the lender can enforce the surrender of the security pledge in court in the event of the borrower's insolvency.

The essential magic trick that has come into implementation with capitalism is that the borrower no longer has to give up something concrete, as in natural barter, in order to be able to obtain something new. Today's people can understand this magic trick using the example of their automobile. For the car, there is both a vehicle registration document, which symbolises the absolute ownership of the vehicle, and a vehicle registration document, which documents the relative natural possessing of the car. If a motorist wants to take out a loan because he additional would like to have a motorcycle, he can deposit the vehicle certificate of property with his bank as collateral for a credit agreement. With the money obtained in this way and the remaining vehicle certificate of the natural possessing, he can still drive the car and also has a additional motorcycle at his disposal. The ideological basis of the credit agreement is therefore the belief in a successful future, or in a

repayment of the credit. (The word credit comes from the latin credo: the faith)
Above all, the so-called compound interest or the interest on the interest is increasingly reaching the limits of earthly nature. The simple calculation example of the so-called Joseph cent illustrates this problem: if a savings account had been opened in the year 0 with only one cent and an annual interest rate of 5%, the balance of the savings book would have grown until today to a value that corresponds to the equivalent of several Earth spheres made of gold.

The transformation of today's economy into a natural economy

A change in today's economic organisation can take place above all through the fact that humans organise the vital house economy and the relatively superfluous luxury economy separately from each other. Since the house economy does not require any major investments and is not associated with a high sales risk, the ensuring of the natural house economy can also be organised by an interest-free exchange money or by a so-called book money. The use of such book money for food supply has already proven to be extremely helpful during the Second World War for the international trade of food.

Interest-free book money has several advantages: Firstly, it makes food cheaper in principle. Secondly, food is no longer subject to stock market speculation, so prices remain relatively stable. Another advantageous side effect is that the food is no longer subject to questionable profit morality. All adults today like to preach to their children that you don't play with food. And yet this is exactly what happens every day on the world's stock exchanges on a large scale. You don't just play with the food, but also with the lives of the peoples affected by poverty. Because as soon as the 'demand' for food increases, the price of food also rises. What this sometimes means for starving peoples does not need to be explained in detail.

The introduction of an interest-free state book money for food today no longer requires any special security deposits, since the state infrastructure in almost all societies is sufficient to insure the book money for the food.

In contrast, a capitalist luxury economy cannot be organised with a simple book money, since there is a much higher sales risk for luxury items than for foodstuffs and usually much higher investments are required.

The separate financial and bureaucratic organisation of the house economy and the luxury economy is a fundamental prerequisite for the successful transformation of todays culture into a natural democracy of symbiotic equal rights. Such a separation enables today's humans to reduce the luxury economy to a level that is compatible with the nature of the earth, without endangering the supply of food to humans.

A gradual reduction of the luxury economy can be achieved above all by analysing all farms above a certain size in detail in order to find out what minimum size these companies must have in order to function and what maximum size they may have so that they do not generate an unnecessary burden on people and on the nature of the earth.

The natural limitation of a person's influence on the community

Each natural species has its own natural boundaries and scales within which it unfolds. This also applies to adults, whose natural growth spectrum is in the range of 1.0 to 2.40 meters in height. In the case of the culture man, the influence on his environment and on the shaping of society is determined not only by his body size, but also by his material and political possibilities and abilities.

In order to be able to realise a sustainable natural cultural organisation, a person's political and material assets must therefore also be limited by a natural from-to spectrum. Otherwise, a natural democracy will always be at risk of turning into a dictatorship as soon as the will of a wealthy few can prevail at the expense of the many.

As cultural history abundantly shows, a unlimited 'private wealth' within a culture leads to a veritable concentration of wealth and thus also to a concentration of the effective influence on the shaping of culture (power) with only a few people.

Since a society is basically nothing more than a living biotope with its own economic cycle of life, an excessive concentration of wealth in a few actors causes a general weakening of the other actors, which inevitably makes the entire cultural biotope susceptible to disturbances. Such a situation represents a serious cultural aberration for several reasons, since the rich and powerful human being, who becomes a 'superman', gives up in an unconscious way his social life insurance through a natural connectedness with the cultural community. More than all other living beings on earth, man is dependent on such life insurance by a social society, since man needs 20 years of maturity until his mental, emotional and physical independence and his nature has no special abilities for an existence as a lone fighter.

The more the 'superman' tries to replace the decomposing natural life insurance with a material life insurance in the form of a supernatural striving for material wealth and for an absolutist power of disposal over other people, the more he gets into a tragic vicious spiral.

People derive an essential security and inner satisfaction from social life insurance, which enables them to relax naturally. A soon as his social life insurance decomposes, an insecurity and dissatisfaction inevitably arise in him that literally gnaw at him. The more the 'superman' therefore strives for a supernatural material life insurance and the more he thereby undermines his social relationships and his social life insurance, the more insecure and dissatisfied he becomes and the more he tries to achieve a solution for his precarious mental situation through an ever more intense striving for wealth and power.

If this vicious spiral reaches a certain degree, then the striving for a material life insurance becomes endemic, so that the 'superman' becomes a 'master man' who tries to dominate the cultural biotope as a whole through an ever-increasing supernatural influence and to modify it according to his 'interests'.
From a historical point of view, it was therefore only a matter of time before the anti-socially organised superman became a master man and the master man became a founder of class culture. To this day, these 'master man' of culture strive in the form of a destructive 'biology' to dominate the entire cultural biotope in an absolutist way.

Today, on the basis of historical reappraisal and scientific research, it becomes clear that even a 'master man' who achieves a strong material life insurance in his life and dominates countless servants and slaves in a direct or indirect way, is never satisfied and can never be satisfied. The deeper reason for this tragedy lies above all in the fact that at the moment when a serious cultural crisis occurs, all the power and wealth of the master man can become worthless, whereby consequently all his relationships dissolve in no time at all. Innate human nature, with its special instinct for self-preservation, is incorruptible and cannot be deceived by arbitrary positivistic interpretations of these facts. Therefore, the unnatural egocentric course of development from man to superman and from superman to master man is doomed to failure in one way or another.

People with social life insurance can survive in the event of a cultural crisis even without power and without material assets, because they stick together and share what they each find in terms of food. Mathematically speaking, 7 people who stick together in one day have far more chances of finding food that is sufficient for everyone than a single person. Not only can they search a 7-fold larger territory for food every day, but they can also succumb animals without firearms in a group. The biological social life insurance that a group of people generates for each group member, even in bitter times, is therefore far bigger than the security that a lone fighter can achieve within a crisis situation.

For this reason, the development of man into a master man has become an extremely tragic development, which today increasingly threatens the fundamental existence of man. Through the invention of class culture and through its progressive development up to the present day, an unnatural cultural curse has arisen for all civilised people. Today's middle-class and lower-class people also increasingly tend to organise themselves through a material life insurance in the form of a lone wolf behaviour. This tragic development is mainly due to the 'practical cultural constraints' that have arisen through the influence of the master man on the shaping of class culture over the last 150 years. Since the turn of the millennium, all 'simple' people have had to fight for their mental, emotional and physical survival in an increasing way. As a result, the cultured person increasingly organises himself in an egocentric way, so that his social relationships decompose in a corresponding way. This inevitably draws a creeping dissolution of the social life insurance of the cultural human being. Many cultured people thereby today have no choice but to strive for materialistic life insurance, as cultural relations are becoming increasingly superficial, non-committal and factual.

It is therefore crucial that today's man realises that he cannot simply replace natural social life insurance with material life insurance without falling into a vicious spiral of a bottomless egocentrism.

Today, through his accumulated knowledge, man can understand for the first time that the 'devil', who has played such a great role in the mythological narratives of class culture, is not a universal being, but symbolises the consequences of giving up social life insurance through the pursuit of material life insurance. On the basis of these real consequences, we can understand that by striving for a material life insurance, man does indeed 'get into the devil's kitchen' because he thereby sells his soul to the culture of class for reaching a fundamental material survival. However, the apparent guarantee of survival of a material life insurance turns out to be a serious trap, as it turns the person into an eternally dissatisfied person who can no longer find inner peace.

It is therefore high time for today's man to understand this grave culturally induced 'destiny' and to actively strive for a natural democracy of symbiotic equal rights. A natural democracy can limit the massive influence of today's 'supermen' and 'master man' on the shaping of societal by means of an obligatory limitation of material and political assets in such a way that these people no longer pose an essential danger to human nature and to the nature of the earth.

The natural restriction of ownership of real estate

The natural territorial right is derived from the natural right of all living beings to occupy a living territory by virtue of their natural self-will and to defend it against external threats. A natural democracy can therefore only grant a natural territorial claim to a person or a family if the land in question is actually used for one's own self-organisation. Of necessity, the current absolutistic property rights for real estate must be restricted in a biological way.

Such a restriction also applies to the economic real estate assets. The size of the buildings used from a company has to be justified by the number of specific workplaces or by the special logistic of the company.

A natural democracy is therefore fundamentally incompatible with the existence of real estate corporations, which have too much power over a natural human existential resource, which can significantly irritate a natural democracy.

Within a natural democracy, the surplus real estate assets, as well as the surplus private assets, go into a cultural structural compensation fund, which primarily promotes natural family ownership and small to medium-sised enterprises. This can not only achieve a fundamental stabilisation of natural democracy, but also a relative economic independence of all administrative districts.

The question of property tax

A family living in their own house or apartment feels biologically safer than a family living in a rented apartment. This perceived security is an important basis for the natural human courage to confront and explore the unknown. For this reason, the ownership of real estate (land and house or apartment) is considered an important means of subsistence within a natural democracy.

Due to such a view, there is no property tax on a person's natural territory in a natural democracy. Today's property tax within the Western cultural sphere is a relic of the medieval feudal system and documents a supernatural presumption of today's state, which grants itself a sovereign right over the entire real estate assets in the culture and taxes this 'right'. For a natural democracy, the property tax therefore represents an unfair interference by the state in the natural territorial right of man and cannot be sufficiently justified by any argumentation.

New forms of economic independence

The Economic Structural Compensation Fund can be used to promote new forms of economic cooperatives within a natural democracy, which are organised financially and bureaucratically by a flexible investment fund. As a result, each member of such a cooperation can contribute his or her natural 'assets' to a corporate investment fund according to his or her abilities, his invested time and his financial share and receive a corresponding monthly profit distribution from the investment fund.

Through the direct financial participation of all employees, the self-organisation of a symbiotic economical co-operative does not require hierarchical command structures. Since all employees are directly involved in the profits of an economic cooperation, they also have a biological interest in making their workplace within the cooperative as effective and successful as possible.

Such flexible economic cooperation can become a new corporate model of a natural democracy, especially if it is psychologically supported by free state health insurance for all acute illnesses. In this way, the risk of the individual for participation in a democratic economic cooperative is kept within manageable limits.
The Economic Structural Compensation Fund within a natural democracy makes another new concept for the promotion of a natural economy possible. By reviewing all bankruptcy filing companies by a bankruptcy administrator to determine whether it is worthwhile to maintain the company for the natural democracy, many valuable resources of knowledge and already existing logistical structures within natural democracy can be maintained.

If it is worthwhile to maintain a bankrupt company, then a special committee can take over the task of working out a new company organisation through a grounding of a democratic investment fund, which will give the former employees of the company the opportunity to take over their former company. Instead of paying employees unemployment benefits or social assistance, all employees receive a share of the new company investment fund, whereby all employees become co-owners of their former company.

Thanks to professional support by the special committee during the necessary handover process, the creditors of the former company can also expect additional compensation after the debt relief process has been completed by the bankruptcy administrator. The prerequisite for this is the consent to resume business relations with the new democratised company. As a result, valuable logistics that has grown over years and decades can be maintained and modernised.

The very fact that the former employees become joint owners of their company gives wings to the motivation of these employees. By setting up a company council, in which the department heads coordinate the company's policy and the respective assignments, the work is enriched by a satisfying social component that can give the new entrepreneurs a new momentum.

By standardising such a procedure for all company bankruptcies through special committees, the respective bodies can ensure that the companies that have gone bankrupt are curtailed in size and logistics in such a way that the newly emerging democratised companies also adequately take into account the needs of the earth's nature.

This bankruptcy agenda can be applied to small companies as well as large corporations, for which natural democracy can grant itself a primary right of exploitation. Here, the process of democratisation requires breaking up the corporations into sole proprietorships, each of which is transformed into smaller democratic companies through the involvement of the former employees. Since all transformed companies are transformed into a living economic organism by means of a heterarchical linkage, today's hierarchically organised corporate groups can also be transformed into democratic single companies through the realisation of a natural line of legitimation from bottom to top.

The natural organisation of society

Today, people can use many open-source software programs that are financed by private donations. Many people are already familiar with Mozilla Firefox, Thunderbird, File Zilla, Open Office and Gimp. All of these programs are free because the programmers have networked in a symbiotic way to work on this software together.

Many of the open source software programs work better in practice than purchased programs, because the philosophy of public benefit behind the programs is far more concerned with the well-being of people than the philosophy of the profit-oriented software manufacturers.

The open-source operating systems Linux Ubuntu and Linux Mint have become respectable operating systems to this day, which already contain a 'service pack' of all important open-source programs. This means that even relatively inexperienced users can immediately start writing letters, surfing the Internet and completing other tasks. How good the Linux operating software has already become can be measured by the fact that it is often used to repair a Windows operating system that is no longer running or to rescue data that is no longer accessible.

A general support through corresponding private donations (crowdfunding) could give Linux its finishing touch, so that Linux can be used for the organisation of a natural democracy of symbiotic equal rights.

Another important open-source objective for a natural democracy is the development of an independent open-source Internet election platform that makes it possible to make visible the real democratic will in a people for a democratic shaping of society. A democratic Internet voting platform would enable every person to cast their vote for important political decisions in their country through a secret voting code, in order to cultivate a new 'Word to Sunday', so to speak. All that is necessary for this is the combination of an open-source Internet election platform with an information platform in the style of Wikipedia, which informs about the upcoming political decisions in culture in an independent way.

Such an Internet election platform would not only be a political school for a democratic cultural design, but also a political barometer for the real political will of the people, undistorted by all commercial interests. This would enable all citizens to orient themselves and to align themselves personally with the real will of the people.

As a result, today's humans can set out on the path to a natural culture relatively independently of the state and of the economy. All that is needed is an active symbiotic networking of all people who are willing to change the way culture is shaped.

Even if such an Internet election platform initially only functions as a political barometer for the will of the people, it is a real blessing for today's relatively disoriented cultural person. The creation of an open-source Internet voting platform is therefore a first extremely important step so that today's human being can set out on the path to a global natural democracy of symbiotic equal rights.

Today, public opinion is formed like in a TV show, so that a few stars and 'experts' play a central role and a mass of viewers follow with 'interest' what views these stars and experts have. The real political power of the individual therefore is limited to a cross that 'The Voter' can make every 4 years on a list of names and parties – a basically poor cult that says nothing about the real political will of the voters. As long as political reality remains so sterile, most people will inevitably organise themselves through the political practice of 'hearing nothing, seeing nothing and saying nothing'.

On closer inspection, the hope that man will eventually have had enough of this kind of cultural self-deception of his own accord is followed by the sobering insight that man has developed an addiction to entertainments that effectively distract him from the unbearable everyday life of today's social culture, so that the political participation remains blocked. This tragic habit cannot dissolve as long as man has no hope of a better alternative.

With an open-source Internet election platform and a corresponding political 'Word to Sunday', the 'ordinary' person can find a way to defuse his current, increasingly unbearable powerlessness in his everyday cultural life and to overcome through an active participation in shaping a natural democracy.

The natural social self-management

Once a national open-source Internet voting platform is used by about 10% of a country's citizens, the agenda of a natural democracy of symbiotic equal rights can be taken to the next level: the formulation and coordination of a catalogue of goals and demands that the peoples can discuss in order to participate in the realisation of a natural democracy of symbiotic equal rights. One of the essential objectives for the realisation of a natural democracy is the implementation of a natural executive with a line of legitimacy from the bottom up, which begins with a direct election of the village and city officials by the respective inhabitants.

This makes local administrators a natural executive authority that organises all day-to-day bureaucratic tasks in a relatively independant manner. Another natural task of the local executive is to align the natural interests of the citizens and the natural interests of the district administration.
As soon as the local administrative officials elect the district officials from among themselves, a first line of legitimacy from bottom to top gets effective. The citizens form the first instance, the local administration the second

instance and the district administration the third instance. Those who leave the local administration by their election as district officials select, for practical reasons, their successors themselves from a list of candidates through personal interviews.

By realising the same procedure for the election of state and federal civil servants, a natural democratic executive emerges that ensures that the citizen has the first and last word in culture.

This concerns not only the organisation of the executive, but also the organisation of the legislature within a natural democracy, since every 4 years the citizens of all districts elect the politicians for the state parliament and for the Bundestag in a direct way with the help of the Internet election platform.

Since the organisation of a modern state is a relatively complex matter, even natural democracy cannot do without full-time politicians. Within a natural democracy, full-time politicians have the task of dealing intensively with the individual cultural fields in order to be able to reach balanced considerations and decisions. They also have the task of presenting their considerations and decisions in their complexity in such an understandable way that they enable citizens to receive a progressive political education by publishing these representations on the Internet election platform. Such a political education initiative is an important component for the realisation of sustainable natural democracy.

The legislation of a natural democracy is carried out both by the Federal Parliament and by the state parliament of all federal states. In order for the bourgeois corrective in the adoption of the laws to take effect, the federal parliament, the state parliament and the citizen parliament each have a voting weight of 33%, with the legislative decisions being carried out via the Internet election platform. This makes the 'Word to Sunday' an important political and social holiday for all citizens.

The remaining legislative voting weight of 1% is conceded to an ethics committee that constantly reminds people that it is important to maintain a biological, empathetic, social and symbiotic attitude. Such an attitude is the icing on the cake of a sustainable natural democracy.

The election of local politicians and district politicians becomes relatively superfluous in a natural democracy, as the citizens themselves shape politics in all villages and towns through their regular 'Word to Sunday'.

The election of judges for the judiciary, like the election of politicians, is carried out directly by the citizen and is in turn limited to the state and federal level. The administrative officials at district and local level organise the district courts in a relatively independent way.

An essential goal of the natural judiciary is that the justice is realised on the natural basis of jurisdiction 'natural law before positive (arbitrary) law'. The judiciary of the federal and state governments therefore has the task of developing new regulations for the replacement of the current jurisprudence basis 'positive law before natural law'. The new legal bases ensure that the natural rights of people, village communities and urban communities enjoy a primacy in cultural jurisprudence.

For all cases in which danger is imminent, the judiciary of natural democracy must develop emergency regulations that are able to maintain public order in the event of a crisis. Such an emergency order is necessary to prevent panic and allergic reactions, which can suspend the natural thinking of humans and overlay them in such a way that great damage can result. As in the natural (primitive?) self-organisation of the tribes, the cultural communities need a leader in cases where danger is imminent (natural disaster, war, etc.), who is provided with extraordinary powers to ensure joint action in such cases. For safety's sake, this is done through honorary positions that are already awarded in normal times, so that they can gain immediate authority in extraordinary times.

The offices of the mayor, the land president and the federal president are particularly suitable for this purpose, which enable the rapid formation of a special Internet committee for the decisions and measures to be implemented in times of emergency. These adopted measures are published on the Internet election platform and are therefore familiar to the entire population in a short time. For the period in which the emergency ordinances remain effective, the emergency committee is obliged to take into account the complaints and suggestions of citizens published on the Internet election platform.

In order to allow the extraordinary decision-making power of the executive required by the emergency ordinances to come into force, an urgent legislative resolution is required that achieves a 2/3 majority of votes. For the decision to repeal the emergency ordinances, on the other hand, a simple majority is sufficient. This completes the fundamental structuring of a natural democracy of symbiotic equal rights. Through such structuring, a sadistic or narcissistic human behavioural derailment within the culture can be prevented at any time by an effective 'resist the beginnings' by the lack of approval of the people. This organisational security is an important prerequisite for todays man's meagre trust in his nature and in his cultural community to flourish again. If this spiritual healing process reaches the degree of a new basic trust in culture and in life, then natural democracy becomes a happy democracy.

The natural global cultural organisation

Once enough nations begin to organise themselves through a natural democracy from bottom to top, humans can take the agenda of a natural democracy of symbiotic equality to the next level: the elaboration of a global Internet voting platform by an already established open-source organisation for example through the Mozilla Foundation. This enables the citizens of all natural democracies to formulate their demands for a global natural democracy in a effective public way.

This creates a Citizen Barometer for global politics, which enables all people to realistically assess the political will of people in the world. On such an independent basis of information, a common global political will can be formed by all people, which can achieve a great assertiveness.

The more nations organise themselves through a natural democracy and the more people participate in the UN election platform, the sooner there will be a real direct election of UN officials and UN politicians, in which all people in all nations of the world can participate in a direct way. A corresponding global 'word to every 1st Sunday of the month' has the potential to initiate a global democracy of symbiotic equal rights and to stabilise it progressively.

By supplementing the UN election platform with an open-source political encyclopaedia in the style of Wikipedia in the most spoken world languages, every person can contribute to the global cultural world increasingly transforming into a happy cultural world through his or her growing knowledge and political participation.

Other important political and economic objectives for a sustainable natural democracy

In order to be able to stabilise a natural democracy in a sustainable way, the implementation of the following cultural regulations is necessary: 1.) The reduction of the average school and working hours to 25 hours per week. This leaves all children and adults with sufficient time and energy for a natural fulfilment of their social needs. A 25-

hour week also enables people to pursue their individual interests and actively participate in the culture politically.

2.) The realisation of a basic free health insurance for all citizens, which can be extended by a supplementary insurance for a fee. Basic health insurance through one's own society promotes an important basic trust in culture and the courage to be self-employed. Especially for small entrepreneurs and for members of economic cooperatives, basic social health insurance is a valuable moral support. A basic social health insurance already exists today in Denmark, Portugal and other countries. In a natural democracy, such basic insurance is relatively easy to finance, as a important goal of a natural democracy is a mental, emotional and physical health of all citizens. One of the main reasons for today's relatively high rate of illness in class culture is that many people lack symbiotic interpersonal relationships. Many lonely older people therefore go to the doctor today with comparatively minor health problems in order to receive the human attention they lack.

The many addiction developments within today's social culture can also be traced back to an unnatural and unbearable everyday life in the class culture. Therefore, this not inconsiderable cost factor for today's health insurance companies will also be obsolete with the realisation of a natural democracy of symbiotic equality. Today, the citizens of the Federal Republic of Germany spend 1.5 billion euros on over-the-counter preparations for colds alone, although a real effect of these remedies could not be sufficiently confirmed by science. We can therefore assume that it is above all the patient's belief in these remedies and only limited extent the remedies themselves, that work wonders here. As long as a culture ignores or even promotes such behaviour in the interest of a 'liberal-capitalist' profit economy, health care necessarily becomes a cultural field in which fear-mongering, unrealistic promises, lies and profit-thinking are commonplace. This unfavourable mixture of facts is another significant cost factor for today's health insurance companies.

The realisation of a natural democracy of symbiotic equal rights therefore eliminates many of today's cost factors for social health insurance. Therefore it is relatively easy for a natural democracy to finance a basic health insurance .

3.) The organisation of empathetic social welfare for all citizens. The social assistance of a natural democracy fulfils above all the important psychological function of strengthening the trust of the individual in the cultural community. This requires basic social security in emergencies, which takes effect in the first 12 months without any conditions for help seeking people.

The abuse of such social assistance by individuals cannot be ruled out in principle. However, the basic trust of all people in their own culture is so important that the principle of 'in case of doubt for the accused' applies to the social welfare of a natural democracy.
Through such natural social assistance, the respective person in need of help has enough time to find a new solution for his or her own self-organisation. This can be done by accepting a new job, by participating in an economic cooperative, by another self-employment

promoted by culture, or by subsidised participation in an alternative self-sufficiency community that gets by on a small budget.

Only after the expiry of 12 months a intensive cooperation of those affected is demanded, whereby the aid funds are progressively reduced the longer the help lasts.
Such flexible social security does not mean blackmail for people, but an emphatic motivation for a natural, largely independent way of life organisation.

4.) The financing of the future old-age pension is increasingly becoming a problem child for the cultures today, since due to the increasing concentration of private power and wealth in all societies, too few financial resources are available to cover the rising costs of pensions.

In almost all natural communities that have been studied by anthropology in the last 150 years, the organisational model of a 3-generation family has been established, which serves an important biological purpose. The relationships between the grandparents and the grandchildren usually have a special quality, since the grandparents are not directly responsible for the children and have wisdoms of life that the parents of the children often still lack. The relationships between grandchildren and their grandparents are usually characterised by a carefree intense love that is enriching for family life.

In this context, it is interesting that the phenomenon of so-called menopause only exists in humans and pilot whales.

In both cases, the grandmothers each take care of their grandchildren in a special way, so that science today assumes that menopause diverts the woman's attention from her own reproduction in order to transfer it to her own grandchildren in the sense of holistic natural family logistics.

A natural democracy does not produce a class war, a generation war, a family war and a war of the sexes which have been 'normal' in the class cultures in the last 5000 years. The transformation of today's culture into a natural democracy of symbiotic equal rights can therefore avert the threat of future poverty in old age for many pensioners today, contribute to a noticeable relief for families and lead to a happy holistic family life.

Natural self-defence and cultural war

Human self-criticism is basically useless if the respective thinking or behaviour that the person concerned criticises is caused by a cultural constitution that is unbearable for human nature. Many people today understandably criticize themselves for their 'conservative', all-tolerating culture-subservient behaviour. However, they cannot change this as long as they are not aware of the underlying cultural mechanisms, which exert a extremely unsettling effect on all cultured people.

Through its unnatural and asocial cultural design, the class culture causes numerous natural and supernatural aggressions in the cultured person, for which those affected usually find no outlet or only an antisocial outlet through the use of scapegoats. For this reason, most cultured people push their natural and supernatural fears and aggressions as far as possible into the subconscious. This creates an extremely dangerous unnatural potential for aggression in those affected, which can break out in the form of a real explosion and get air in an extremely destructive way.

The supernatural aggressions that man develops within the culture of class today nourish various antisocial vicious circles in culture, which are realised in the form of outright wars. The culture of class therefore not only generates supernatural cultural aggressions, but it also 'cultivates' these cultural aggressions in a regular way through regular internal theaters of war: the war of the estates, the generational war, the family war and the war of the sexes.

These conflicts represent the primary wars of class culture, as they are constantly in progress. The wars that the class culture wages from time to time against other class cultures are to be regarded as secondary wars for several reasons. Sometimes the secondary wars also arise from the fact that the internal primary aggressions of two class cultures have reached a degree that makes an external aggression valve necessary so that the affected class cultures do not destroy themselves.

In addition to the internal wars of culture, which have become a veritable outlet for the supernatural fears and aggressions of cultured people, man today also cultivates sports that are particularly suitable for reducing aggression, such as the modern martial arts and the rough physical sports (rugby). These sports allow not only the fighters and players, but also the spectators to discharge their inner aggressions to a certain extent.

In the field of music, too, we find an art form today that reduces aggression in a effective way, the so-called rap. The rap uses an aggressive gutter language to generate a special aggression valve. One analyses the lyrics of this music, it quickly becomes clear that the rap achieves its special impact through a sexualised sado-masochistic language of the aggressive kind, since the famous 'f...' word triggers a stimulating kick in the human mind. Since rap has also been adopted to a certain extent into the everyday language of the younger generations, rap today generates a constant sado-masochistic sexualization of everyday cultural life. Even though rap offers an effective cultural aggression valve, the sado-masochistic sexualization of song lyrics causes a progressive distortion of the human mind and soul through an unnatural abuse of the sexual impulse force.

Any cultivation of a supernatural aggression outlet for the culture-caused aggression is always only a short-term emergency solution, but not a long-term solution. A lasting solution to the underlying problem can only be achieved by eliminating the causes of the supernatural cultural fears and the cultural aggressions. How full of consequences the suppression of the supernatural aggressions of the culture person into the subconscious can become became clear above all through the Vietnam War, which has been extensively documented by the media. For a long time, many Vietnam veterans had to struggle hard with what had become of them in the

Vietnam War, sadistic and cruel warriors, which could not restrain their violence even against women and children.

We find these 'normal side effects' of the war in the last 5000 years sufficiently confirmed by the reappraisal of cultural history. Above all, the downright rape of 'enemy' women in the course of a war sheds special light on the nature of these inhuman culture caused aggressions, which find their outlet regularly in the wars.

The master men of all class culture have always used the derailings of supernatural human aggression to maintain the class culture in a psychological way . To this end, they accuse the nature of man a fundamental bestiality and justify the necessity of a dictatorial class culture in the form of an absolutist state constitution.

As we know today, the problem of the supernatural aggressiveness of the cultured man is not solved by this, but intensified in an increasingly way. It is mainly for this reason that man today is confronted with the danger that he will destroy himself if he continues further to maintain his self-organisation through a culture of class.

It is the war that makes monsters out of humans and it is the class culture that generates wars with many faces. Those who have understood this no longer blame human nature or the 'animal' nature of man for the cultural phenomenon of a constant war against everything natural. It is rather the class culture that transforms humans into unnaturally organised humans.
It is therefore of essential importance that today's man learns to distinguish between the natural war over vital

possessions and the supernatural, usually senseless wars of class culture.

Only then will it become clear to today's human being that the realisation of a natural democracy of symbiotic equal rights inevitably produces an enormous redemptive effect for all human beings, since supernatural fears and aggressions no longer accumulate in human beings, which lead to a constant unnatural wars in the cultures and between the cultures. A natural democracy therefore becomes for man a place where real peace instead of today's periods of armistice is getting normal.

Therefore, even if the global military situation today is such that no one wants to confront this grotesque situation anymore, this is no reason to abandon all hope in man. Man is quite capable of ending the arbitrary and destructive nonsense that class culture produces today.

As soon as a sufficient number of nations organise themselves through a natural democracy of symbiotic equal rights, the UN can get on the way systematic global disarmament and meaningful recycling of all global war equipment through a democratic legitimacy.

The elimination of today's environmental overloads

Since the nature of the earth is already in a precarious state, man can no longer wait for the UN to organise itself through a natural democracy of symbiotic equality. It is therefore important that everyone is sufficiently informed about the problem areas of global environmental overload. In this way, all people can contribute to a certain extent to progressively reducing today's overloads of earthly nature.

The renewal of the humus layer on the arable soils

Over the last 60 years, industrial agriculture has removed too much of the top humus layer of arable soils. As a result, many soils have been transformed into humus-free steppe soils, which can only be cultivated with artificial fertilisers. Today, a reconstruction of the natural humus layer with already available microorganisms through a targeted use within 5 years is possible. One of the advantages of such a global renaturation of soils is that around 19 billion tonnes of CO2 can be bound globally in the new humus layer. This can improve perceptible the Earth's climate balance.

Reducing the particulate matter problem

Today's air pollution caused by the so-called particulate matter is largely due to industrial agriculture. In its studies on air pollution in Germany, the Max Planck Institute has measured the share of industrial agriculture in particulate matter pollution at 45%. The removal of humus soils, the use of large harvesting machines and the use of fertilisers, insecticides, herbicides and fungicides create a sometimes extremely dangerous mixture of fine dust, which is partly responsible for the development of the most recent diseases of civilisation. It is therefore an important concern that humans avoid herbicides, fungicides and pesticides as far as possible in the future, because this creates a dangerous particulate matter from which no one can protect themselves. Depending on its size, particulate matter can fly up to 500 kilometres.

In recent years, many farmers have severely restricted or completely abandoned the use of herbicides, fungicides and pesticides. This has been made possible mainly by the fact that many experiments in alternative pest control have been successful, above all the settling of natural predators. Even the experiment of setting up nesting boxes for barn owls around a field against a special form of rats was successful. In order to be able to settle the respective predators of pests, a flower strip in the form of a demarcation of the arable fields is necessary. By planting berry bushes, fruit trees and various plant species, a generally favourable environment for insects can be created. By studying the needs of the natural predators of the respective pests, a permanent settlement of these predators can be reached. Thereby the flower strip that borders the fields becomes a worthwhile holistic natural project. Many projects of this kind have paid off financially, as the cost of chemical agents can be greatly reduced and a green strip prevents the loss of arable land during heavy rainfall. The long-term gain of fruit and berries likewise pays off in the long term in view of today's relatively high fruit prices.

The targeted reduction of species extinction

In addition to limiting the agricultural arable land with a green strip of shrubs, fruit trees and flowers, the promotion of allotment garden associations and smaller farms is also a way to strengthen the animal and plant world. An application in one's own municipality to leave some of the municipality's meadows to the nature can also produce valuable results. As soon as meadows are not fertilised with nitrate (slurry), the natural spread of fungal threads (mycelium) in the soil creates a natural basis for life for many plants and insects that have become rare today. If a new colonisation with these plants and insects takes place, then even birds that have already become rare can find a suitable breeding area again and settle.

The cleaning up of the world's oceans from plastic and the recycling of plastic

To date, 5 large plastic whirlpools the size of France and Germany have formed in the world's oceans, so scientists assume that more than 170 million tonnes of plastic have accumulated in the world's oceans. Again and again, larger plastic particles are found in the stomachs of whales and seabirds and the so-called microplastics are found in mussels, fish and humans.

Since we have had a technical process for more than 20 years that enables us to produce biodegradable plastic from natural fibres, there are several starting points for achieving feasible solutions for the ever-increasing plastic problem.

Today, humans are technically quite capable of constructing special ships that remove the coarse plastic waste from the world's oceans.
In order to rcduce the use of plastic in principle, a decentralised supply of fruit and vegetables in all districts is important, which also does not require plastic packaging.

The general recycling rate of plastic in Germany today is 15% on average. In most cases, downcycling takes place, so that, for example, flower pots and park benches are made from plastic bottles.

The central problem for the recycling of plastic and for the generation of plastic waste arises from today's packaging habits, as food is often packaged in several types of plastic or by a combination of plastic and aluminum. If the consumer does not conscientiously separate the different types of plastic and the aluminium from each other and cleans them before they go into the yellow bins, there is usually no plastic recycling and the plastic is incinerated with household waste.

In order to achieve an acceptable recycling rate for plastic, it is necessary to limit the types of plastic to a maximum of 5 types that can be easily recycled. By clearly labeling these types of plastic, they can be collected separately from each household. As soon as only one type of plastic is permitted for an outer packaging, which may at most be combined with a packaging material made of cardboard or aluminium, but not with a packaging material made of another type of plastic, a real recycling rate of 75% to 95% can be achieved for each of the 5 permitted types of plastic by means of a professional cleaning system.

Cardboard packaging and paper is already 95% recycled. There is also already an effective recycling process for certain aluminium alloys. By massively reducing the aluminium alloys used, a satisfactory recycling result can therefore also be achieved for the raw material aluminium.

The plastic problem is not only a national problem, but a global one, as there are no recycling processes in many countries today. The more nations organise themselves through a natural democracy, the sooner the global plastic problem can be solved by the UN in a nationwide way.

The protection of the rainforests

The rainforests of the earth not only form the lungs of the world with their oxygen production, but also influence the climate of the earth. The aerosols produced in the rainforest ensure the formation of raindrops, so that the rainforests create a self-regulating microclimate that ensures abundant rainfall and heavy cloud formation. The rainforest is therefore not only an indispensable oxygen supplier for all terrestrial life, but also an important air conditioning system for the earth.

Despite all the warnings that have been issued for 40 years regarding the need to protect the rainforests, man has already cut down a big part of the rainforests for industrial food production and for the extraction of raw materials and is as before reducing the rainforest every day.

Here, too, only the UN can ensure in the long term that the rainforests are preserved and transformed into nature conservation zones through a global economic structural compensation fund.

The restriction of factory farming

Modern factory farming of cattle endangers the future viability of humans in many respects, as the methane emissions of the animals promote global warming on earth and large areas of rainforest are cut down for the food of the animals.

In addition, modern factory farming is increasingly tugging at the conscience of humans, as many animals in factory farming lead such an unnatural life that the corresponding image and documentary material is sometimes difficult to 'digest'.

The pictures show tattered chickens from factory farming, which sometimes have ulcer-like bumps all over their bodies. Many chickens lie half-dead on a layer of feces in a confined space in large warehouses where there is a constant loud background noise. This makes it vividly comprehensible to the viewer why many animals in factory farming are kept alive with antibiotics.
Such animal husbandry is not only a constant ethical problem for humans, but also a biological danger, as the regular administration of antibiotics promotes the

development and spread of so-called superbacteria. These are mainly bacteria that are resistant to various antibiotic preparations. If people become infected with such superbacteria, then survival becomes a matter of luck, as there are only a limited number of antibiotic preparations available.

It goes without saying, therefore, that a natural democracy of symbiotic equal rights cannot accept such conditions in its own culture.

Further considerations

Most of the current overloads of nature by humans can be mitigated in a relatively short time. However, it has been shown that the problem areas of the environment can mutually potentiate each other, so that for some of the problem areas there is little time left until so-called tipping points are reached due to the overlapping overloads of the natural circulatory systems, at which the regulatory framework of the natural system cycles is suspendet. Like an overturned pond, this leads to the system circuits becoming chaotic and remaining unpredictable for a while until a new progressive order can emerge again.

Of the approximately 100,000 artificial substances produced by the chemical industry to date, about 800 substances influence the hormonal balance of animals and humans. If chemical substances with an estrogenic structure get into the water, this leads, among other things, to male fish becoming womanised in the rivers, or to frog species no longer being able to reproduce because the frogs' mating call changes.

The production of 1 million tonnes of plasticizers and the production of 400 million tonnes of the plastic bisphenol A are are today held partly responsible for the fact that many young men are found to have drastically reduced sperm activity. Specific studies have also found that the plastic bisphenol A is associated with diabetes, obesity, thyroid disorders, developmental disorders in children and with infertility.

The long-term effects of the 100,000 chemically produced plastics are still largely unknown. This is mainly due to the fact that only simple series of tests have been carried out for the developed substances in order to determine the degree of stress at which animal cells react with a disease. To this day, it has not been taken into account that a simultaneous interaction of different chemical substances can result in potentiated effects on a cell or on an organism.

For human future viability, it has therefore become advisable to reduce the chemical substances used to a total of 1000 substances, so that it is possible to complete sufficient test series that also investigate the simultaneous influence of different substances on the living organism. This is the only way to maintain sufficient food safety and rich biodiversity in the long term.

Today, many corporations have become global nomads who check every step of their production to see where and how the products can be produced most cheaply. This is usually done via double and triple transport routes, so that many products travel a long way by ship across the world until they are completed. The costs of this neoliberal logistics are borne by nature, as marine diesel pollutes the environment in a considerable way, in contrast to car diesel.

A large number of modern consumer products are now manufactured in more than 200 special export centres around the world, which have been constituted as special zones and where duty-freedom, low taxation, permissive environmental standards and 'liberal' labour laws apply. As a result, products can be produced at dumping prices, as wages, which are usually paid in the export centers, are below the respective subsistence level of the country. In order to avoid responsibility for these production conditions as far as possible, many corporations no longer produce under their own name and on their own account, but commission independent companies within the export centers to produce the desired goods.

The relative passivity of modern man in relation to the dangers of liberal-capitalist environmental overload, which are becoming increasingly obvious today, makes clear that modern man organises himself not in a sane way. The common man must therefore learn to accept the fact that he can no longer simply place his life in the hands of the cultural authorities. In the last 35 years, the neoliberal agenda has led to the fact that the interests of nature now rank third behind the interests of 'the economy' and behind the interests of man. Man can only end this tragic kamikaze course of today's class culture through a conscious unification from below, by actively working for the realisation of a natural democracy of symbiotic equal rights.

The natural science

We know today that even the small hoverflies have a unique, individual nature, so that there are no two identical hoverflies. Therefore, we can say that the individual is the essential mode through which natural life on Earth is realised. This makes it necessary to declare the scientific demand for an objective view of life, which has remained valid to this day, an unnatural, sterile demand, since the subjective and thus the actually living is largely left out of scientific consideration.

Since the Industrial Revolution, science, which tends towards objective perfectionism, has developed a cold, antisocial busyness, so that to this day it no longer makes any distinction between medical laboratory tests, the production of war technology or the realisation of a 'holistic' digital surveillance technology. Thus, with regard to objective science, we can also speak of an ethically and morally dead science in order to better understand how it could come about that man has developed hydrogen bombs with which he can blow up the nature of the earth several times.

Cultural history, therefore, teaches us that the scientist, more than any other human being, must be able to evaluate the fruits that his work generates for humanity. If the scientist lacks a subjective, empathetic perspective for his field, then he necessarily becomes a dangerous person for human society.

The current state of science and technology therefore makes not only the personal natural responsibility on the part of the scientist and technician necessary, but also a special attention of the society to the science and the technology through a ethics committee elected by the citizens indispensable.

Chapter 3
The biological philosophy

Through the invention of class culture, man has increasingly neglected his natural thinking, feeling and acting and replaced it with arbitrary thinking, feeling and acting. In order for man to be able to dissolve the destructive cultural symptoms that have arisen as a result, he must above all reflect again on his innate capacity for symbiotic empathy. Through such an empathy, man can gain new insights that have remained hidden so far.

The natural empathic relationship

The natural social relationships of humans are basically a simple bio-'logical' matter. They require an empathy for each other's individual self-organisation, which is done primarily by putting oneself in the other's shoes. Such an empathy requires a relative selflessness for the period of empathy, since only in this way is it possible to be absorbed in the reality of the other and to 'understand' the other. This inevitably means that a happy symbiotic relationship can only be sustainable if both partners interact and take care of each other. Without such social 'logistics', a relationship is only an egoism in pairs, but not a natural 'relationship' of companionship, friendship or love.

The natural relationship is and remains the essential means of organisation in evolution, so that the human being can only learn something if he relates to a fact, to a fellow human or to the respective circumstances in an empathetic way. In doing so, people always carry out what we call identification. Through identification, the human being registers and 'scans' not only the respective external appearance, but also the inner essence of a state of affairs or a person with its respective complex peculiarities and imports the holistic impression of it in the form of pictures, feelings and thoughts into his consciousness. Without such identification, a relationship remains merely superficial interest. Therefore, if the human being is not 'absorbed' in the facts, in the other or in the circumstances, he does not live in the natural sense but only performs the ritual of variety, which remains relatively insignificant.

Many people today have only a vague interest in life and entertain each other through superficial relationships, which have become 'normal'. This fundamental curtailment of the natural gift of life is a result of class culture, since its military machine, its economic machine and its bureaucratic machine can only be maintained by a superficial, relatively sterile and indifferent reference of the cultured man to their respective functions in culture.

So it is that for 5000 years the cultured person has been oriented towards abstract rituals and artificial ideals, which the individual does not fathom in depth, because he only holds on to the form of these rituals and ideals for a 'successful' adaptation to the culture. A biological examination with the content of these rituals is important, because it leads to the realisation that these rituals are completely arbitrary and ultimately serve an unnatural purpose. This will remain the case as long as a cultured person limits himself to repeat what is ideological standard in the culture. Such self-organisation is not life, but rather a living death, since those affected by it are basically not really touched by anything and over time fall into the habit of 'normal' passivity, irresponsibility and indifference.

Recognising the enormous difference between a natural reference and a mere interest is therefore one of the essential prerequisites for the human being to realise and sustainably maintain a natural democracy of symbiotic equal rights.

The unnatural relationship habits of today's culture people

As a rule, one does not need to explain to an empathic person that a happy human self-organisation is only possible through an empathetic reference to life, but not through organisational concepts that realise only a superficial interest in life. This includes also the concepts of selflessness and egocentricity, which both lead to a relative sterility in relationships. These relationforms have an extremely detrimental effect, since the human being nourish through his natural symbiotic relationships of the empathic kind a basic trust in life. This sense of security is the prerequisite for the natural courage that man needs to venture into every new unknown life situation.

A class culture that takes its children the natural will, the natural empathy and the natural courage as a prerequisite for successful 'adaptation' to the culture, is inevitably not a sustainable culture. The affected cultural people are missing something essential in their lives. They develop only an artificial or superficial 'interest' in life and tend to become indifferent and disrespectful to life as such.

The good business and the scapegoat

How dangerous the superficial interest in life of a cultured person can become for a society is illustrated by today's neoliberal 'interests' of the corporations, through which the 'legal person' of a corporation sometimes acts so insolently, disrespectfully, antisocially and parasitically that man has become a danger for the entire natural evolution of the earth. There is therefore no reason why today's person should respect the 'interests' of the 'legal person' and the shareholders, since in doing so he pulls away himself the natural ground under his feet in an indirect way.

As long as there are capitalist people who pat those people of their 'guild' on the back who have succeeded in making a 'good deal' - no matter how this business has come about - the human species and the nature of the earth stays acutely endangered. Today, the 'good business' still includes 'ripping off' other people, parties or companies. The correspondingly 'successful' human being is still referred to today as a 'devils guy' and through a grotesque sympathy a member of annvisible Olympic discipline of a 'liberal-parasitic' capitalism. A culture that tacitly allows such 'successes' inevitably has no future worth living.

Another devastating everyday organisational cultus of today's class culture is the unwritten 'permission' to vent all supernatural aggressions, which arise within the culture on scapegoats.

Today, this no longer happens through a conspicuous physical violence, but through a invisible passive-aggressive ideological and emotional violence. Since the culture aggressions pass on from top to bottom in a sadistic way, it has become proverbial that the last in this series 'are bitten by the dogs'.

These 'last' are each the children of the lower culture classes, which often become members of a regular 'underworld' within the culture. In its ideological, emotional and physical use of violence, the cultural underworld acts just as excessively as the class of the 'master men' in the culture.

This creates a threatening pincer movement for the common people through a 'liberal-parasitic' acting master man and through a 'liberal-criminal' acting 'underworld man'. The essential difference between the master men and the underworld people today is that the influence of the master men on the formation of the class culture reaches so far that they no longer have to use obvious violence. In the last 70 years the obvious power of the master men has increasingly been transformed into indirect cultural constraints. Thereby the resulting existential pressure remains passive-aggressive and is despite this very effective. As a result, the rule of the 'master men' remains largely unreflected in today's class culture.

The frivolous use of scapegoats for a cultural 'hygiene of aggression' has considerable consequences for all people in today's class culture. Those who recognise this for the first time usually throw their arms up in disbelief, so perfidious is the resulting degenerative 'cultural logistics'.

Most of the social problems of today's society result therefore from an unnatural and asocial cultural organisation and are not caused by human nature. There is, therefore, no natural reason why today's man should not be able to organise himself through a natural democracy of symbiotic equal rights, that dissolves all the destructive behavioural and relational symptoms of today's class culture.

The natural education of children

As early as 2500 years ago, the Greek philosopher Heraclitus formulated the maxim for a natural education of children: 'To teach is to light a fire and not to fill an empty bucket'. Many educators in history have implemented this wisdom in a special way, such as Maria Montessori. As a result, it has been shown again and again that people learn in a sustainable way, above all when they are enthusiastic about what is to be learned. This insight has only arrived in an extremely limited way in the school system of today's class culture, since today's school system primarily promotes and grades the memory performance of the children in order to educate the students according to the goals and interests of the capitalist class culture.

Today's social culture needs a constant supply of well-'adapted' cultural servants for the functioning of its absolutist cultural machines of the military, the economy and the bureaucracy. These can only be produced by an unnatural upbringing, since man possesses very special talents and abilities for creativity and freedom, the cultivation of which is a natural need for man. It has therefore become important for the simple cultural person of today to consciously distinguish between the natural interests of human nature and the supernatural interests of culture.

The invention of childhood

With the development of a regular Pietist school education by August Hermann Francke (1663 - 1727 AD), a first cultural concept for a regulated childhood and a new educational and school pedagogy in Europe emerged after the Thirty Years' War from 1618 to 1648. The new pietistic pedagogy included the goal of breaking the natural self-will of the children in order to be able to better adapt the children to the cultural requirements. This 'Black Pedagogy', which has developed progressively in Europe over the centuries, promoted in the children above all a strict self-discipline, a constant self-optimisation in the sense of culture and an absolute obedience to all cultural authorities.

In the course of the Industrial Revolution in the 19th century, normal 'liberal-parasitic', sado-masochistic and tyrannical relationships emerged within the capitalist class cultures, so that the 'adult world' was increasingly characterised by extremely asocial behaviours. Among other things, this led to children from a age of 4 being called upon to do industrial work and sometimes being overstrained to such an extent that mental, emotional and physical malformations were the result. Therefore, in Europe and America from 1850 onwards, the concept of childhood was taken up again and strengthened, so that a 'puppy protection' was created for the children in order to protect the children from the 'seriousness of life' within the normal world of adults.

Since the turn of the millennium, the children's closed season established in the cultural world has increasingly dissolved, especially due to the freely available information on the Internet, since today children are confronted with the reality of the 'adult world' at a relatively early age. As a result, the younger generations are becoming increasingly disrespectful towards adults due to their current experiences and knowledge, which were not accessible to them until the turn of the millennium.

Children and adolescents who are confronted too early with the sado-masochistic relationship world of adults usually suffer a social shock, so that they remain trapped for a long time in a mental state characterised by psychological conflicts, excessive fears and feelings of disgust.

This is an extremely momentous experience for children, as children are fundamentally dependent on their parents. This makes the 'normal' parent-child relationships in today's class culture correspondingly difficult.

Gustave le Bon drew attention to the consequences of this normal childhood experience in his book 'Psychology of the Masses' as early as 1895: [...] 'At all three stages of instruction in childhood, boyhood and adolescence, theoretical preparation at the school desk and from books has been prolonged and overburdened, with regard to the examination and the academic degree, the diploma and the application of an unnatural and anti-social course of education, the excessive postponement of practical teaching by the boarding school, the artificial drill and the mechanical overfilling of memory, by neglecting the real world into which the young man will soon enter, the society that surrounds him, to which he must adapt.

This indispensable equipment, this achievement that is more important than all the others, this efficiency of common sense, will, and nerves, is not won in our schools; on the contrary, instead of making man more capable, they make him unfit for his immediate and future position. Therefore, after leaving school, his entry into the world and his first steps in the field of practical work are nothing but a series of painful defeats, from which he emerges wounded and for a long time worn down and crippled.

It is a kind of a dangerous trial in which the spiritual and moral balance is shaken and runs the risk of not being restored. The disappointment came too abruptly and too completely, the deception was too great and the disgust was too strong. The education given to today's generation justifies the darkest premonitions.

Changing this general state of affairs would be a difficult task. One would first have to transform our miserable Roman education. It robs everyone of initiative and energy to whom heredity has left something of it. It extinguishes all semblance of intellectual independence by giving youth as its only ideal a series of hated contests that require only a memory performance and the end result of which is to place at the head of every profession precisely those brains, whose servile ability to imitate makes them completely incapable of individual achievements' [...]

This description of the education realities around 1895 makes clear that the disenchantment of children by entering the world of adults since a long time means a culture shock, which has considerable consequences.

The only realistic solution also for this cultural problem is to work with all available forces towards the realisation of a natural democracy of symbiotic equal rights. Through the realisation of a natural democracy, today's sado-masochistic relationship world of adults dissolves as if by itself and gives way to an equal symbiotic relationship world. Thereby the danger of culture shock for the children is cancelled.

The 'education' of reward and punishment

Since 2500 years the culture of class is drawing a monotheistic God in heaven, who has the characteristics of a tyrannical authority and who extorts people to a God-pleasing behaviour through a pedagogy of reward and punishment.

After the Thirty Years' War from 1618 to 1648, a 'black pedagogy' became normal in European culture, which transferred a divine authority to the pedagogical educators. The consequence was that the pupils were 'domesticated' by a 'self-evident' use of mental, emotional and physical violence in the sense of culture.

This pedagogy, which emerged after the Thirty Years' War from 1618 to 1648, is today referred to as 'Black Pedagogy' because its arbitrary pedagogy of reward and punishment primarily pursues the goal of breaking the natural self-will of the children at an early stage.

To this day, the pedagogy of reward and punishment has remained normal in the class culture and is practisised through a passive-aggressive ideological and emotional manipulation. The real consequences of such an education are made clear above all by the modern 'good cop – bad cop' game of police interrogation methods. The rollercoaster ride of hope (reward) and fear (punishment), which there is applied, uses up the human nerve strength in a relatively rapid way and leads the interrogated person into a real capitulation.

The education of children through a passive-aggressive pedagogy of reward and punishment also results in a 'capitulation' of the children to the educators in the long run. It is therefore to be regarded as a psychological method of breaking the natural self-will of the children and replacing it with the will of the educator.

Therefore, as soon as parents today become agents of the class culture and apply the educational method of reward and punishment to their children, an unnatural ideological weapon is used that leads the child into a chronic weakness of will. Experience shows that the child's self-will that remains after such a pedagogical education can be superimposed and controlled relatively easily by all authorities and 'experts' in the culture.

Of necessity, a person whose natural self-will was broken in childhood remains a shadow of himself and tends to be psychologically dependent on an impulse and 'will-giving' external authority throughout his life. It is therefore self-evident that such child-rearing is unthinkable within a natural democracy of symbiotic equal rights.

The modern racism of intelligence

In the last 70 years, the modern class culture has developed a new racism that is realised through an evaluation of human intelligence. This new variant of a human classification works in a hidden and yet effective way.

The French sociologist Pierre Bourdieu (1930 -2002) took a closer look at this modern racism of the intelligence and found the following: [8][...] 'In my opinion, it is very important to analytically deal with those forms of racism that are probably the most subtle and difficult to recognise and are therefore also the least criticised. Perhaps because the ordinary critics of racism themselves have some characteristics that make them susceptible to this forms of

---

8. Book; Pierre Bourdieu “Sociology in Question“

racism. I mean the racism of the intelligence. The racism of the intelligence is a racism of the ruling class, which differs in a whole series of characteristics from what is usually called racism, that is, from petty-bourgeois racism, which is the main target of the classical critique of racism.' [...]

'The racism of the intelligence is what the rulers use to try to produce, as Weber [9] says, a 'theodicy of their own privileges', that is, a justification of the social order they dominate. It is this that gives the rulers the feeling of being justified in their existence as rulers; the feeling of being beings of a higher kind.

All racism is an essentialism, and the racism of the intelligence is the characteristic form of the sociodicy of a ruling class whose power is based in part on the possession of titles such as educational titles, which are considered a guarantee of intelligence and have taken the place of the old titles such as titles of property and nobility in many societies in access to positions of economic power.' [...] 'The racism brought to a very high degree of euphemization in this way is almost no longer recognizable.' [...]

Of necessity, every racism and every idealistic class formation remains a danger to the self-organisation of man, since these are absolutist hierarchical divisions of people that inevitably progressively degenerate all symbiotic relationships in a society.

---

9. Max Weber Sociologist (1864-1920)

For the relative nature of man, the skin colour, the race, the religious affiliation and the education of a person are and remain necessarily only relative, but not absolute characteristics and therefore do not justify an absolutist hierarchical categorisation of people. The class culture, which only functions with an absolutist and hierarchical ideology, tends to evaluate not only the class, but also the skin colour, the race, the religion and the education as absolutist characteristics. The resulting arbitrarily generated scale of values leads to a corresponding value categorisation of people. Such a ideologic division of society serves the class culture for the application of one of its essential formulas of power: 'divide and rule'

In the book 'The Technopol' by Neil Postman we find a detailed debate of the intelligence test in use today, which has become a motor for the racism of the intelligence: [10]
[...] 'A thorough analysis of the fatal role of statistics in the 'measurement' of intelligence is contained in the great book 'The Wrongly Measured Man' by Stephen Jay Gould. I would like to refer here only briefly to three points discussed at length by Gould:

[…] 'The first problem is reification, the transformation of an abstract idea (usually a word) into a thing. In our context, the reification works as follows: With the word 'intelligence' we designate a variety of human abilities that we consider favourable or desirable. A thing called 'intelligence,' on the other hand, does not exist. 'Intelligence' is a word and, on top of that, a word on a high level of abstraction. However, if we mistake them for

---

10. Book: „Das Technopol“, Neil Postman, S. Fischer Verlag GmbH, 1992, S.141ff.

a thing such as the pancreas or the liver, then we necessarily come to the conclusion that she can be localised and measured by scientific methods.

The second problem is the creation of rankings. This requires a criterion with the help of which each individual can be assigned a place on a single scale. And, as Gould says, what could be better suited for this than a number? So when we assign intelligence a place in a ranking, we assume that intelligence is not only something material, but is also a single thing that is located in the brain and to which a number can be assigned.' […]

[…] 'After E. L. Thorndike had spent a lifetime measuring intelligence, he found that intelligence tests have three shortcomings: What they actually measure is not known; to what extent it is permissible to add, subtract, multiply, divide or calculate proportions of the measurement results obtained is not known; what the measurement results actually say in terms of intelligence is not known.' […]

[…] 'And Joseph Weizenbaum wrote: There are few 'scientific' theories that have thrown the thinking of scientists and laymen into more confusion than the theory of the 'intelligence quotient' or 'IQ'. The idea that intelligence can be quantitatively measured along a simple linear scale has done unspeakable damage to our society as a whole, but especially in the field of education.

Gould has documented some of this damage, and Howard Gardner has tried to reduce it in his book Frames of Mind. But the technopoly resists such accusations, because it needs the belief that science is a completely objective undertaking. Lacking clear ethical principles and rejecting tradition, the technopoly is looking for a new source of authority and finds it in the idea of statistical objectivity.' [...]

Human intelligence is realised above all through an empathy for a certain fact, for a living being or for the respective circumstances. For this reason, the vernacular also likes to speak of emotional intelligence. Such intelligence is not to be evaluated, as it has to take into account too many individual factors from which no objective values can be derived. Therefore, the attempt to measure human intelligence and ascribe an individual value to it contradicts the nature of science.

A natural democracy of symbiotic equal rights therefore rejects the absolutist evaluation and categorisation of human intelligence by means of a division of scales, just as it rejects all arbitrary divisions of people into castes, classes and estates.

The healthy natural psyche

Over the last 100 years, modern psychology has in-depth analysed the psychological aberrations of humans in the modern class culture. As a result, we can now establish in a relatively reliable way that people develop downright behavioural disorders within a class culture, that the roots of these behavioural disorders go back to early childhood and that many disorders can be traced back to so-called traumas. We can also understand these traumas simply as experiences that are unbearable for human nature.

Modern brain research has shown that the mental, emotional and physical self-organisation of the human being is organised by 3 special areas of the human brain, the brain stem, the cerebrum and the cerebellum. The brain stem ensures the basic survival of humans in a instinctive way, the cerebrum organises a constantly expanding awareness of the world, develops the capacity for natural reason and organises the social relationships of humans. The cerebellum increases the efficiency of human self-organisation through a habit formation that automates regularly recurring thought and action processes, such as walking or piano playing.

Since its inception, the class culture has been organised through 3 cultural machines formed by humans: the military machine, the economic machine and the bureaucratic machine. In order for these machines to function smoothly, class culture needs the selfless 'machine man' who can put his natural self back or deactivate it to such an extent that he does not become a disruptive factor for the hierarchical organisation of the respective cultural machine.

This can be achieved above all by parents in the class culture passing on their already developed abilities for selfless cultural adaptation ('The culture is everything, the individual is nothing') to their children through an appropriate education. A regular school education and an apprenticeship in the world of the economic machine then do the rest, so that the children of culture still become cultural citizens today, capable of a masochistic self-discipline and a self-dictatorship.

The unbearable authoritarian education and its consequences

Children who grow up in an authoritarian family constellation usually develop supernatural behavioural strategies at a very early age in order to avoid or neutralise all unbearable family relationship experiences as far as possible. The anticipatory obedience practiced by the children in a regular way is often seen by the parents as a success of their educational style, so that parental education tends to develop a progressively intensifying authoritarian educational system of the sadistic or narcisstic kind.

The child adapts to this destructive development of parental behaviour, since it has no other choice, and thus develops a correspondingly compliant behaviour in order to maintain a relative harmony in the parent-child relationship.
This creates a tragic, mutually firing sado-masochistic parent-child relationship, which tends to turn the parents into master men and the children into subservient beings of an alien will. Sooner or later, the tragic 'progress of this sado-masochistic relationship constellation leads to an overload of the children's natural psyche. This leads from time to time to a momentous panic reaction in the children to the behaviour of their own parents.

Panic is a special behavioural programme within human self-organisation in a situation, that is perceived as life-threatening, which switches off the thinking and concentrates all forces, to achieve a release of the situation through a panicked flight or an allergic reaction.

However, a child is so dependent on his family that he cannot react to a panic attack in relation to his parents without serious consequences such as an allergic reaction or a panic flight, since each of these two reactions further exacerbates the emergency situation that has arisen for the child.

A child who instinctively expects protection and support from his parents, but develops a panicked reaction with regard to the behaviour of his parents, experiences what we can call an extremely contradictory, 'hellish' state, because the bottomless fear of survival that sets in in the child as a result shakes the child's basic trust in life. If a child experiences such conditions more frequently, then a allergic reaction to its own parents can develop, which inevitably means a catastrophe for the child's mental balance.

A child affected by a panic or allergic reaction does 'EVERYTHING' to prevent such a state of soul. Accordingly, the child feverishly searches for a solution, so that for this purpose it also copies and tries out the behavioural roles of all people tangible for the child through the natural instrument of identification, in the hope of finding a solution.

The child finds what it is looking for as soon as it copies and tries out human behavioural roles that realise a absolutist selflessness. The resulting experience that within the state of a supernatural selflessness the biologic rule 'Where there is no I, there is no pain' takes effect is experienced by the child as a redemption.

In the course of time, the child supplements the thereby resulting artificial cultural ego with further behavioural roles that largely reduce social relationship conflicts, so that over time they cultivate a whole complex of self-contained supernatural and unnatural behaviours. As a result, the natural self is banished to the subconscious in a sustainable way.

Without realising it, the child becomes increasingly dependent on external impulses and artificial motivations, as his abilities for a natural self-organisation and self-motivation progressively decrease. This is mainly due to the law of natural economy, which reduces all abilities in a living being that are no longer in regular use. The inevitable effectiveness of this law is made clear by a broken leg, which shows a significant muscle atrophy after the plaster cast has been removed.

As a result, many children of culture develop an unconditional obedience to all cultural authorities at a relatively early age through a notorious selflessness. This development is usually reinforced by the fact that the affected children also take up the ideal of selflessness proclaimed and heroised by the traditional cultural religion of class culture in order to stabilise and idealise their selfless self-organisation in a progressive way. This religious trap is still a danger for all children of culture today.

Any attempt by a selfless child who has grown up to transform a notoric obedience to all authorities into a natural behaviour again is prevented by a inner psychological cerberus. Because as soon as the adult tries to return to his natural self, there is a so-called 'trigger effect' that reactivates his own childhood experiences of the hellish kind and the associated panicked and allergic constitutional states.

The lifting of a selfless obedience to authority is therefore a hard nut to crack for many of those affected. Those affected need a psychological support for such a resolution, which takes the edge off the problem. This can also be moral support from the social environment, which encourages the affected person to withstand the emerging 'trigger experiences'.

Essential for a resolution of the trigger effects is the awareness of those affected that the unbearable childhood experiences have arisen from a unnatural parental behaviour and from the fact that a child is fundamentally and holistically dependent on its parents. The emerging trigger experiences therefore relate to the situation of a relatively powerless child, but no longer to the current situation of the child who has become an adult. This insight can help reduce the sharpness of the trigger experiences.

As a rule, the resolution of the trigger experiences is aggravated by the fact that a child who is allergic to the behaviour of his parents represses his panic and allergic reactions in order to be able to put a good face on the sadistic or narcissistic behaviour of his own parents. In this respect, too, the child has no choice. For many affected children, this turns family life into a permanent mental and emotional game of hide-and-seek, which is always associated with the fear that the parents will notice that the child is engaging in a special supernatural way of mimicry.

For this reason, the affected children usually demand a 'impeccable' behaviour from themselves in an absolutist way, whereby the children develop a correspondingly iron self-discipline and self-control of the dictatorial kind. This inner dictator must be dissolved by those affected, as it can effectively prevent the deconstruction of panic fears, allergic reactions and the ability to a overnatural positivistic mimicry.

It is helpful for those affected to keep in mind that they are not the only ones affected by this problem, as it is a normal cultural phenomenon. On the other hand, it is important to realise that humans can only sufficiently organise messages and relationships that correspond to their nature.

Therefore, all supernatural, unnatural and unbearable experiences and ideas remain unprocessed present within the psychic self-organisation of the human being. They can therefore cause from time to time a psychological irritation within the mental or emotional self-organisation.

The tragedy that has been cultivated by the civilised human being for 5000 years in the class culture consists above all in the fact that the attempts of the civilised person to develop any compromise or any successful behavioural strategy for an adaptation to the class culture always fail because of the unnatural constitution of the class culture and its inevitable consequences.

Many of the supernatural psychological fears, aggressions and problems with which man has to struggle today within a class culture that has become extremely 'effective' therefore dissolve slowly but surely as if by themselves through the realisation of a natural democracy of symbiotic equal rights.

The natural relationship between the sexes

Another obstacle that today's man must overcome in order to achieve a stable natural democracy of symbiotic equal rights is the pacification of a war between the sexes that has been raging for 5000 years, which today distorts natural human sexuality in an extreme way.

The natural self-organisation of humans is characterised by a complex family logistic, the biological meaning and purpose of which is above all to ensure the long and difficult maturation process of the children. As a rule, humans underestimate the great and special effort that human reproduction represents. This starts with the fact that the large brain volume of the human child has not only led to a change in the female pelvis, but also to special birth logistics. In contrast to all animal cubs, the human child is born much too early. Therefore, a child only reaches the level of physical maturity about 2 years after birth that an animal cub often features immediately after birth. A horse foal for example can get up half an hour after birth and follow its mother.

Since a child, unlike an animal, can no longer fall back on a large part of the animal instincts, the child must develop a natural world view and an individual self-organisation for its orientation. A human therefore always learns everything in a new way. Especially this has made it possible for humans to adapt to all climate zones on earth.

Since a child is more or less completely dependent on the mother for the first 3 years, we can consider the family as an invention of human nature that serves a successful reproduction of man. This assumption is underpinned above all by the fact that women and men develop strikingly different characteristics, abilities and preferences. These abilities predestine the man for a natural family foreign policy and the woman for a natural family domestic policy.

Since we find a bio-'logic' for everything in nature and nothing is realised by nature without a good reason, we can conclude from the complex reproductive organisation of humans that family formation, as well as the formation of a social village community, is indispensable for humans. It is therefore not without reason that the vernacular of many peoples says that it takes a whole village to raise a child.

We can conclude from this mixture of human self-organisation that human sexuality, which in contrast to most animals remains constantly active, fulfils a specific purpose and does not exist for humans to amuse themselves in an arbitrary way. Rather, it can be understood as a necessary natural reward and as a source of motivation for a strenuous human 'reproduction business'.

Such a conclusion is reinforced by the fact that humans have no fur and their skin has very special sensory cells that only react to cuddles. These special social and sexual rewards are a natural insurance for successful human reproduction.

Human sexuality, like the sexuality of animals, is organised in a not inconsiderable way by animal instincts. Therefore, with regard to the constantly active sexuality of man, nature has constituted an effective protection against an arbitrary inflammation and degeneration of human sexuality, the so-called natural shame. The shame usually only dissolves naturally when a couple has gained trust in each other and an increasing natural passion opens the way to sexual union.

Human sexuality should always be treated with caution, as it constantly has the same assertiveness as animal sexuality during the rutting season. This rutting season is characterised by an irresistible sexual union that ensures an offspring. The power of sexuality ensures the preservation of species even then, if there is a lack of a concrete will on the part of those involved. The natural sexual organisation therefore involves a certain power of command.

Since natural sexuality is constantly active in humans, it is also relatively easy to ignite a sexual fire in a representative of the opposite sex through a shameless gigolo behaviour or a coquette behaviour. A passionate assault of the ideological and emotional kind on the natural fortress of shame of the opposite sex is often sufficient for this.

The strong influence that sexuality can have on a person's behaviour is made clear above all by the proverbial sexual humour, which is able to forgive everything and effectively clears the way for a sexual union. Sexuality should therefore be treated with caution due to its natural assertiveness, even for modern people. The sexuality can cause enormous damage to all interpersonal relationships, especially within today's class culture, in which people are increasingly looking for overnatural motivations.

For this reason, it is important that mothers and fathers in particular keep reminding themselves that the special constitution of human sexuality serves to preserve the family and ensures the natural maturation process of the children. Human sexuality is therefore by nature not a permissive product of pleasure that is intended as a consolation for an unnaturally and unbearable organising class culture. The sexuality is part of a complex natural family organisation that must be respected, since the sexes can hurt each other deeply and seriously through an arbitrary disregard for this organisation in the form of sexual frivolity.

Above all, these 'normal' mutual violations of the sexes in the class culture have led to the start of a gender war 5000 years ago, which rages today more than ever in all class cultures and ensures a fundamental mental and emotional separation of the sexes.
Many people today harbour a bottomless anger in relation to the opposite sex. We find the beginning of this seemingly indomitable rage already in the early advanced civilisations through the implementation of a veritable sex slavery.

Slavery is characterised by a complete deprivation of rights and by an arbitrarily generated powerlessness of the people concerned, which is enforced through the use of a bottomless ideological, emotional and physical violence. As a result, the sexuality of the slaves became a commodity that could be given away or sold. Thereby the natural shame of sex slaves was declared null and void and destroyed. Thereby the natural shame of sex slaves was declared null and void and destroyed. As a result the invention of sex slavery became the beginning of a culturally determined, unnatural and shameless prostitution.

Since the city-states in Mesopotamia have repeatedly waged wars over the water rights on the Euphrates and Tigris rivers, the male 'warrior' with his physical strength became a cultural ideal in Mesopotamia. The exaggerated glorification of male physical strength has led to women being seen as a 'weak sex' in Mesopotamian culture and being devalued in a fundamental way. As a result, a veritable patriarchy arose in Mesopotamia, which was characterised by an unnatural absolutistic power of men over their wives.

In the the German book: Milestones of World History - Advanced Civilisations on the River, we find the following note:[11] [...] 'Single and married women were entitled to a number of important rights under Sumerian law. They were able to acquire their own property, conduct business themselves and appear as witnesses in court. In other respects, however, they were treated as

11. Citation: Book Meilensteine der Weltgeschichte Hochkulturen am Strom, Weltbildverlag 1999, P.26

second-class citizens. Therefore male succession applied in the family, in other words, the property passed from father to son. And the rules of marital cohabitation seem to have been quite one-sided. The husband could, by law, have one or more concubines, disown his wife if she remained barren, and even sell her into slavery for a period of up to three years to pay his debts.' [...]

Through this arrangement, the woman in Mesopotamia became a relatively impotent part of the Mesopotamian family organisation. Such a 'slavish' relationship, which is constituted by a relative omnipotence on the one hand and a relative powerlessness on the other, becomes what modern man understands by a sado-masochistic relationship. Such a relationship is characterised by the absolutist control and dictatorship of the ruling relationship partner which inevitably becomes over time sadistic, so that a'master man' arises, who develops an overnatural sadistic lust of power over other people.

The controlled relationship partner develops a masochistic self-control of the absolutistic kind and a constant passiv-aggressiv selflessnes so that he can survive psychologically and physically. Over time, he developes a perverted masochistic lust for success through his increasing abilities of absolute self-control and of a permanent self-dictatorship. This self-organisation, like the self-organisation of a 'master man,' can also become tyrannical.

To this day, people have not sufficiently realised that the emergence of an unnatural sado-masochistic relationship sets in motion a dangerously destructive relationship development. The unnatural sadistic relationship recipe of the master man and the unnatural masochistic survival recipe of the slave man complement each other in a tragic way. Thereby arise a devil spiral of progressively intensifying violence in the sadomasochistic relationship.

Sooner or later the relationship enters a crisis. Since a sadistic behavioural norm is an unnatural and bottomless behavioural agenda, many man and today also women develop a sadistic addiction to power, which can transform the sexuality and generate many perverse male and female behaviours. This also includes the already more than 3000 years old phenomenon, that the winners of a war rape the women of the defeated people.

The emergence of a male sadistic power addiction and a sex addiction opened up for women the possibility of a supernatural influence on men which could be generated above all by a sexualised body language. Since not only the female slaves and the prostitutes, but all women gradually practiced a supernatural manipulation of male, the females thereby were able to alleviate their relative powerlessness in culture.

The answer of the class culture was a division of the official cultural roles of women into the role of the whore and the role of the saint. As a result, an increasing sexuality of the purchasable kind was promoted in culture, while the sexuality in the families was increasingly reduced to the concrete act of procreation. At this point, the relationship between the sexes became a question of power and less and less a question of natural love.

The more women in the class culture began to manipulate and challenge men through a 'skillful' sexual body language, the stronger the man's fear of this supernatural (witch-like) behaviour became and the more drastically the woman was suppressed by men and the patriarchal class culture.

The first historical peak of this spiral of violence in gender relationships can be found in the Greek city-states from around 600 BC: women were largely banned from public for the first time and had to cover their bodies in public. Thus, the slight inflammability of the sadistic male sexuality, which had become 'normal' within the class culture, was no longer exposed to the supernatural temptations of a 'liberal' female 'body language'.

Since the turn of the millennium, this traditional 'cultural policy' of class culture has increasingly turned into its opposite. At the same time, the natural shame of the human being has been almost completely dissolved by the modern media. Since then, more and more women are cultivating a sadistic addiction to power and a sex addiction, which have extremely destructive consequences.

The role of the whore as well as the role of the saint overwhelm and violate the nature of women in a bottomless way to this day. Just as with the invention of slavery, the culture of class has 'cultivated' an unbridled underlying anger in the affected people through the invention of patriarchy. Like the slave, the woman also had to suppress her inner anger to survive in the patriarchal class culture. Only those who empathically comprehend this can understand why the kitschy idealisation of a women as a selfless saint became an enemy-picture for the feminists of the 20th century.

The natural woman is neither a whore who sells herself for money, nor is she a saint, but a natural being who can only find her happiness and inner peace if she can live in a symbiotic and thus equal way in the cultural community. Only in this way the natural respect and love of man for his neighbour arise in a happy way.

It is the biological task of the man to protect the family from external destructive influences. The man has failed in this in the last 5000 years, because he has allowed himself to be corrupted by the 'interests' of the class culture and bribed for an absolute power over the woman.

Since the turn of the millennium, the women makes increasingly the same mistake. With the cultural transformation of patriarchal family law into a matriarchal family law at the turn of the millennium, the women has not used physical violence for the desired social change in culture, but ideological and emotional means of violence that have successfully imprisoned the man in a longing and sex addiction. This does not result in happiness either for the gender relationship or for today's families.

It is becoming increasingly clear that both women and men must consciously emancipate themselves from the cultural model of class culture. Only in this way can the woman and the man defend their natural social relationships in a sufficient way against today's class culture, which is increasingly developing into a cancer for all life on earth.

However, as long as the citizen waits in the sense of the absolutist religious constitutions of the class culture for a transformation of the culture to be blessed from above, both the woman and the man stand in the way of a real transformation of the class culture into a natural democracy of symbiotic equal rights.

The natural religion

Humans are born with a reduced instinct programme, which is why children must gradually develop an individual view of the world in order to be able to organise themselves in a successful way.

The human worldview is composed on one hand of what man has gathered through his experiences and through his scientific findings in terms of reliable knowledge. On the other hand man On the other hand, people need a belief in the relatively unknown causes of all the inexplicable things in life so that they can build a holistic world view.

Religion is a part of the human belief system that focuses primarily on the existence of the universe and the nature of the invisible world. The word religion comes from the Latin religio, which designates the act of referring back to something. We can therefore understand religion as a reference back to the universe and to life.

Such a reference back to life can, as in the case of many primitive peoples, lead to a veneration of animals and their special characteristics, whereby experience shows that the power of animals is admired above all. A religion can also be shaped by the idea of a heavenly world in which, as in the Greek world of gods, the same relationship dramas take place as in the human cultural community. A religion can therefore also be designed as a social mirror in the form of a transfer of the own existence into a supernatural world.

All religious ideas remain harmless as long as they are designed in a relative way and the gods or the drawn figures do not generate a threatening effect on the believers. If a threatening religious effect arises, then natural religion becomes an unnatural religion and can cause considerable damage both in the personal and in the community organisation of man.

The abuse of religion in the class culture

From about 2500 BC onwards, religion was abused in the city-states of Mesopotamia in a veritable way to educate the cultural citizens in the sense of the cultural military machine, economic machine (temple building) and bureaucratic machine that had emerged up to that point to become submissive citizens.

In a natural community, there is no reason for the individual to organise himself through a unconditional obedience to leading personalities in the community. For a class culture, however, selflessness and obedience to authority on the part of the ordinary citizen are prerequisites for the cultural machines to function smoothly. This is particularly evident today as before, above all in the cultural military machine. Without unconditional obedience to authority, the hierarchical organisation of the military machine would not function.

For this reason, already the early class cultures developed a cultural religion that is still characterised by 3 essential objectives today:

1. The creation of a general supernatural fear of the civilised people of absolutist heavenly gods

2. A blind unconditional obedience to the gods and the governors of the gods on earth (god-kings and priests)

3. The creation of a supernatural sense of guilt towards the gods and the cultural governors of the gods.

How such a religion was designed in the early city-states is documented by an evaluation of the clay tablets discovered by archaeologists in Mesopotamia: 'According to Sumerian belief, the gods had created the earth's inhabitants from clay because they needed slaves to serve them. Anyone who failed to worship them and appease them had to reckon with misfortune, floods, droughts, plagues or raids by the mountain tribes. And since the Sumerians were indeed not infrequently afflicted by such plagues, they lived in constant fear of their gods. This made religion a dominant force – and brought enormous advantages to the temples. The only way to avert divine wrath was to bestow abundant donations on the granary of the temple and to obey the commands of the priests.' [12]

---

12. Quote Book: Meilenstein der Weltgeschichte-Hochkulturen am Strom, Weltbild Verlag 1999 S. 13

This fundamental psychological constitution of the early cultural religion exists to this day. Above all, the religious phrase of 'guilty obedience' is still many people today a term. Accordingly, the inner blockades of many cultural citizens are still strong today as soon as a critic of the behaviour of the authorities in the culture has become necessary. This is also truc cven if such criticism, as is the case today, becomes necessary for survival. This phenomenon is mainly due to the supernatural feeling of guilt, which religion has been planting in the world view of the cultured people for 5000 years.

The generation of a supernatural sense of guilt arises primarily from the unnatural use of the natural social sense of guilt of all people. A natural social sense of guilt always arises when a relationship becomes imbalanced due to a one-sided taking or giving and threatens to be seriously damaged. Since humans are more dependent on the social life-insurance of society than all animals, an unpleasant feeling of guilt arises in those affected as soon as one of their social relationships gets into disharmony.

This social relationship logistics of human nature is exploited by the culture of class in an unnatural way, in that it persuades man of a social relationship debt towards God and thus also towards the God-willed cultural authorities. This can also occur in a subtile way through the belief that God sacrificed His Son for the sins of man. Through the principle of action 'constant dripping wears away the stone', such a religious interpretation of guilt achieves a resounding effect on all believers over time.

A person who adopts a supernatural religious belief in guilt has to struggle with serious inner conflicts as a result. These conflicts stem from the fact that man is confronted with feelings of guilt, the resolution of which depends on an arbitrarily acting God and on equally arbitrary acting governors of this God on earth. In this regard, especially in the Christian religious constitutions, we find again and again the reference to an eternal debt of man towards God. This proclamation of eternal guilt is the crucial ideological building block for the emergence of a constant supernatural human sense of guilt. Such a sense of guilt can be 'milked' by the authorities of the culture in various ways. One of the most well-known and extreme forms of this use was the medieval indulgence payments to the Catholic Church, for which the believer received a written guarantee in the form of a letter of indulgence.

As a rule, the religious pressure mechanisms of a class culture are not sufficient to produce a lasting capitulation or unconditional obedience of the faithful. Every human being has a living urge for freedom by nature and therefore cannot simply decide on an absolutist obedience to authority. Therefore, after an initial phase of adaptation to the class culture, there are outbreaks of inner anger in the affected citizens.

Since the governors of God on earth declare these irascible outbursts to be the evil in man par excellence and describe the irascible human being as a being that is possessed by the devil, a serious inner insecurity arises for those affected, since such an accusation endangers their social security.

The 'accused' therefore try to stop their outbursts of irascibility through increasing self-control and self-dictatorship, whereby their inner mental and spiritual state increasingly deteriorates.

If it comes to the point that a person affected can no longer maintain the suppression of his supernatural fears and aggressions, so that the outbursts of anger become more intense, then the 'proof' of the existing evil in the person concerned is also confirmed for the person concerned himself. The resulting threat of complete loss of social life insurance and self-control is usually frightening enough for the person concerned to capitulate once and for all to practice a blind general obedience to 'the will of God' and the will of the cultural authorities.

Overall, we are dealing therefore with the religious staging of a psychopathological development through a bottomless, arbitrary and deeply antisocial blackmail of the ideological kind. This kind of bottomless social blackmail is usually necessary so that a person gifted with a special ability for natural freedom becomes an obedient citizen, which works for the cultural machines of class culture as requested.

This systematic psychological breaking of the cultural bourgeoisie reached its first psychopathological climax in Western culture with the Inquisition in the Thirty Years' War from 1618 to 1648, since in the Thirty Years' War countless 'sorcerers and witches' were burned not only in the Catholic, but also in the Protestant areas of power, who had 'the devil in their body'.

In a 'bio-logical' sense, the irascibility is the consequence of a repressed allergic reaction and, like the emergency programme of panic and the allergic reaction, therefore has no natural limits. Therefore, a person who is unaware of the nature of irascibility may stumble upon an arbitrary religious interpretation that mistakenly rates irascibility as an expression of evil and condemns it accordingly.

Since every natural religious measure was exceeded in a bottomless way during the Thirty Years' War, after the Thirty Years' War a 'black pedagogy' was established in Western culture, which broke the natural will of children very early, usually before the age of three. This made it possible to educate the children of the culture in a relatively inconspicuous and extremely effective way in favour of the supernatural demands of class culture.

As late as 1965, there were parenting guides in Western culture that recommended simply letting the baby cry in order to break the 'tyrannical' will of the children.

The problem with the religious concept of chosenness

The concept of religious chosenness first appeared in the Jewish religion and developed into a serious Jewish problem in the history of the Jews. Today, on the basis of historical research, we can assume that an allergic reaction of the Jews to their captivity in Babylon was an essential reason why the Jewish founders of the religion were able to lay the Jews an absolutist monotheistic religion successfully to the heart. The newly created god of the Jews was far more powerful than all the other gods of that time. As a result, the detail of the new belief, that the monotheistic God declared the Jewish people to be his chosen people became a strong new hope for the Jews of their liberation from Babylonian captivity.

This liberation finally took place and led to a lasting anchoring of the new belief in an omnipotent monotheistic God in Jewish culture. The many tests that the Jews had to pass according to the Old Testament in order to stay connected with their new God have painted the picture of an absolutist, tyrannical God who wants to educate people to be godly people through an 'educational' reward and punishment.

For this, the Jewish God did not hesitate to subject the Jews to tests of the sadistic kind (e.g. a demanded sacrifice of one's own son). Such a God was inevitably capable of evoking in the believing Jews both a lasting supernatural fear and a stable supernatural enthusiasm. This supernatural polarisation of the Jewish religion has remained to this day the most powerful weapon of all monotheistic religions, as they can thereby bind the faithful permanently.

The act of faith that made the Jewish people the 'chosen people of an almighty monotheistic God' was able to motivate the Jews greatly on the one hand, but on the other hand it brought them much suffering. Since the Jews were with such a faith much more recalcitrant to the absolutist claims to power of the Romans than other peoples, they lost their ancestral homeland in 70 AD.

This event resulted in a diaspora that lasted 1875 years. During the time of the Diaspora, the belief in their 'chosenness' helped the Jews to stick together and survive a history marked by many denunciations and religious persecutions.

The ideological concept of 'chosenness' has a dark consequence, the isolation and alienation from other communities and people who cultivate a different faith. The belief in being the chosen people of a single almighty God has inevitably reduced or degraded all other peoples to 'unchosen' peoples in the Jewish world view. This has given rise to a hierarchical religious thinking within Jewish self-organisation, which has inevitably strained relations with all 'unchosen' man and peoples.

A hierarchical value division of people through the ideological concept of chosenness also becomes clear in an underground way through the language, the facial expressions and the gestures of the elect. Therefore, for the Jews, the religion of Judaism became a blessing of a religious elixir of survival, a curse of exclusion and a constant enmity trough other ethnic and religious communities.

Not only the awareness of being chosen, but also the many extraordinary religious precepts of the Jewish religion prevented a simple assimilation of the Jews in Christian countries. As a result, for a long time the Jews in the Christian sphere of influence were only allowed to stay in certain areas and only to engage in special professions, such as trading in gold, diamonds and slaves or the operation of a credit system. All these transactions were considered disreputable in Christianity, which is why they were forbidden to Christians for a long time. This created another involuntary 'chosenness' for the Jews within European Christianity, which led to the beginning of a special European monetary and financial system.

Since many Jews became rich through it, the Jews occupied from the 17th century onwards in an above-average manner the higher cultural positions in the European culture (doctors, artists, scientists, etc.) . This 'chosenness' in turn brought with it a bitter 'fate' for the Jews, as the Christian alienation over the religious rites of the Jews and the relative Jewish isolation began to mix with an increasingly bottomless envy of Christians for the Jewish wealth and the Jewish positions in culture. This eventually led to disastrous pogroms and persecutions of Jews throughout Europe.

The idealist concept of chosenness is therefore an ideological construct that is extremely explosive and destructive in many respects, as it can fuel absolutist separatism and absolutist competitiveness and drive it to ugly destructive extremes.

This tendency is also evident today in the general relations of the monotheistic world religions with each other. Despite the fact that all three monotheistic world religions are based on the Old Testament and refer to Abraham as the common progenitor, the monotheistic world religions have not yet succeeded in finding friendly interaction, since every religion to this day tends to insist on its own 'chosenness' in a absolute way.

Not only the Jewish religion, but also Christian Calvinism has emphasised the divine chosenness in a special way. Due to the belief concept of predestination, which is valid for the Calvinist religion to this day, every human being is either a person 'chosen' by God or an 'unchosen' human being.

This religious conception played a special role in the development of capitalism in Eropa and Amerika. With regard to the divine division of man into chosen and not chosen people the Calvinism assumed, that the chosenness of a person is revealed by the material situation and by the cultural position of the respective person. As a result, a special striving for influence, power and wealth became normal in the countries that were influenced by Calvinism, like Prussia, Switzerland, France, Holland, England and America.

The Calvinist religion regarded the cultural authorities as fundamentally appointed by God and prohibited the disobedience even with regard to the 'strangely' behaving cultural authorities. As a result, a particularly rigid pursuit of material wealth and elevated social positions was 'normalised' in european countries and later also in America through a special mixture of calvinism and protestantism.

After the Thirty Years' War from 1618 to 1648, the Prussian kings were all raised by Huguenots, French Calvinists who had been expelled from France and had found a new home in what is today Brandenburg. The Prussian virtues of thrift, diligence, punctuality and honesty can be traced back to this Calvinist influence. We can therefore speak of a great influence of the Calvinist religion on modern cultural formation. Today, only a few people are adequately aware of this. Therefore the striving for success, for perfection and for everything absolute, overnatural and sensational has remained an unrecognised and extremely harmful fruit of European religious history, which continues to keep the 'liberal' capitalism alive.

For the liberal capitalists, all religious fantasies about being chosen and about one's own universal specialness are still more important than the nature of the earth and the morbid state of the soul of the 'unchosen' humans. Since in America both the Calvinist 'chosenness' and the Jewish 'chosenness' get united in the American capitalism, an extremely antisocial and unnatural economic and financial aristocracy developed in America in the 19th century. Since the turn of the millennium this financial aristocracy strives in a progressive manner, to suspend all ethical and moral boundaries in culture for an absolutist global capitalism. As a result, America (God's own country) has tended since the turn of the millennium towards the realisation of a global Calvinist governorship of God on earth.

Since 1985, the 'chosen ones' (rich, powerful master men) have been waging a war against the 'not chosen' (poor, powerless workers) in all Western cultures, through which cultural power is increasingly centralised and monopolised. The resulting 'material culture-constraints' transform the interpersonal relationships slowly but surely into sadomasochistic master and slave relationships. The 'chosen' will win this war against the 'unchosen' if the common man does not recognise what a sick religious game the culture is playing on every new day. This game ends inevitably with the result, that all humans will become losers.

The religious metaphysics

Even though religion is a matter of faith, people can use metaphysics to develop a relative natural worldview with a high degree of probability. Above all, the following physical findings give individuals a basic vision of the nature of the universe:

1. The universe organises itself in a relative way. Since Einstein published his theory of relativity, many scientists have tested and confirmed this theory, so that it is now considered secure.

2. The statement that the universe expands like an organism in a regular way is also considered secure.

3. The universe has a special fractal ordering principle that enables man to recognise the relative order of nature in all organic living beings on earth.

4. The so-called gravitational constant applies to the entire universe. Therefore the gravitational force is in the whole universe the same and ensures also the stability of our solar system.

5. The discovery of a natural multi-level organisation with a relatively self-sufficient self-organisation of the various

levels through the system research enables us to better understand the universal nature.

6. The univers is organising itself through a general polarity of order (security) and chaos (freedom). Because of this relative polarity there is nothing absolute, perfect and unconditional in the universe.

7. The spontaneous emergence of life on earth from a favourable 'primordial soup' has made it clear to modern humans that life is generated by an impulsive birth process, which is essential for the formation of natural evolution. The universal potency of life, to ignite itself under favourable circumstances and to organise itself in a sustainable way, distinguishes all living systems from all technical systems that the civilised man has developed.

Technical systems always remain dependent on an external entity that specifies all the necessary parameters for the basic structure, the path and the goal of the respective system processes to be carried out. Life emerges through a symbiosis of the smallest building blocks of life, which form cells, organs and bodies and finally entire niches with numerous different life forms. These life forms complement each other and form their own natural life cycle, which can experience evolutionary development.

Since the universe is expanding, we can consider the universe as a whole to be a living organism that organises itself by special ordering principles, by certain laws and by a polar field of tension of the dynamic kind. The resulting living relationships and interactions lead to the fact that life in the entire universe can organise itself in a relatively free, creative and flexible way.

We can therefore understand the universe as a living being that organises itself in a relatively uniform way, generating a holistic universal reality through a multi-level organisation that reaches from the smallest building blocks of the universe to the galaxies. Through this reality, every living being in the universe remains part of a universal being at all times and places.

All human beings today are therefore taking part, without being sufficiently aware of it, in a special universal experiment that is taking place on earth through evolution. In this respect, all people today are chosen people.